Decision-making for New Product Development in Small Businesses

What goes on in a small firm that lives or dies by its capacity to innovate? How are decisions made on new product development, and how does that feed into the ecological, social and financial sustainability of the firm? This book answers the questions through an in-depth look at a small business that manufactures high-end carpet yarn.

Using advanced analytical techniques to interrogate rich qualitative data, the book draws together established theories of decision-making and new product development, coupled with thinking about business sustainability to improve our understanding of this important area of business practice. The book further reinforces the importance and role of organizational learning in organizational decision-making, based on novel analysis of empirically developed qualitative data.

Mary Haropoulou is a Course Quality Officer at the University of Western Sydney.

Clive Smallman is Professor and Dean at the Higher Education Leadership Institute.

Routledge Advances in Management and Business Studies

For more information about this series, please visit www.routledge.com/Routledge-Advances-in-Management-and-Business-Studies/book-series/SE0305

Decision-making for New Product Development in Small Businesses

Mary Haropoulou and
Clive Smallman

Routledge
Taylor & Francis Group

LONDON AND NEW YORK

First published 2019
by Routledge
2 Park Square, Milton Park, Abingdon, Oxon OX14 4RN

and by Routledge
605 Third Avenue, New York, NY 10017

First issued in paperback 2020

Routledge is an imprint of the Taylor & Francis Group, an informa business

British Library Cataloguing-in-Publication Data
A catalogue record for this book is available from the British Library

Library of Congress Cataloging-in-Publication Data
Names: Haropoulou, Mary, author. | Smallman, C. (Clive), author.
Title: Decision-making for new product development in small
    businesses / by Mary Haropoulou and Clive Smallman.
Description: Abingdon, Oxon ; New York, NY : Routledge, 2019. |
    Series: Routledge advances in management and business studies ;
    80 | Includes bibliographical references and index.
Subjects: LCSH: New products—Planning. | Small business—
    Decision making.
Classification: LCC HF5415.153 .H375 2019 | DDC
    658.5/75—dc23
LC record available at https://lccn.loc.gov/2018045598

ISBN 13: 978-0-367-50412-0 (pbk)
ISBN 13: 978-1-138-85505-2 (hbk)

Typeset in Galliard
by Apex CoVantage, LLC

This book is dedicated to our parents (June, Despina, Ken and Kostas), to our children (Christos and Nikos), and to the rest of our family.

Contents

Figures

Tables

Acknowledgements

This book grew out of Mary's PhD thesis, which evolved over several years. The success of that project is attributable to many people. Professor Steve Wratten (Lincoln University, New Zealand) helped with an original concept, which after several months fell through. Despite that setback, Steve supported Mary throughout from the sidelines, giving encouragement and hosting some memorable meals. Associate Professor Misha Balzarova (now University of Canterbury) and Dr David Dean were Mary's supervisors

Clive acknowledges the Routledge team, notably Samantha Phua in bringing the book to fruition, over a protracted period, as Clive changed roles. Clive also acknowledges the contribution of Matt Church, Pete Cook, Stephen Scott Johnson, Chris Freeman and the rest of the Tribe at Thought Leaders Business School.

1   Sustainability, decision-making and new product development

Sustainability defined

This study originated in our personal interests in ecological sustainability in business. This is a phenomenon that excites considerable debate and has done so for some time. Our first contact with the subject came in 1993 in a short course on *Environmental Management in Small and Medium Sized Enterprises* at Bradford University in the UK. The course was developed by Richard Welford, an eminent scholar of corporate environmentalism (Welford, 1996, 1997a, 1997b, 2000), and was amongst the first courses worldwide to address this issue. From that time, research and reporting upon the issue of ecologically sustainable business, has grown almost exponentially (Dunphy, Griffiths, and Benn, 2007).

However, sustainability *per se*, has acquired a much broader meaning in common business usage than the one that is focused solely on ecological impacts. In addition to a firms impact on the natural environment, sustainability is now commonly used in discussion of a business's financial position (Luffman, Sanderson, Lea, and Kenny, 1991; Tirole, 2006) and, more recently a business's position as a good corporate citizen (Banerjee, 2008; Matten and Crane, 2005). This latter development is of course a better reflection of the original conceptualization of sustainability (WCED, 1987).

We follow Costanza (2000), viewing business as an economic production system (Haropoulou, Smallman, and Radford, 2013). This system is a chain of subsystems that extends from the extraction of raw materials through production processing, marketing and sales and eventually to disposal or recycling (Caldwell and Smallman, 1996). In an orthodox economic model this chain is concerned with 'adding' economic value as raw materials are transformed to finished goods. Hence, in its original formulation, the value chain's focus is on the efficient supply of raw materials to efficiently manufacture goods or to efficiently produce services (Porter, 1985) through optimizing an organization's primary activities (e.g., inbound logistics, operations, outbound logistics, marketing and sales, service). In a conventional economic production system, financial sustainability is a principle requirement of continuing to operate any business; ecological and social sustainability are matters of conscience.

In heterodox ecological economics, the focus of the supply chain is on the ecologically sustainable production of goods or service provision. This requires not just optimization of primary activities, but also considered approaches to secondary functions (e.g., procurement, information and production technology services, human resource management, firm infrastructure services, corporate governance and executive management). Ecologically sustainable production extends not just to production processes; through the secondary functions of product creation and development, ecological sustainability may be built-in (McDonough and Braungart, 2002). In Costanza's (2000) formulation, the wider ecological economic model also stresses the importance of returns to physical, human and social capital, accommodating the three elements of sustainability previously outlined.

Radical as it is, the ecological economic model is far from enjoying universal acceptance by orthodox economists or businesses. Moreover, the adoption of ecologically and socially sustainable business practices varies across the world. However, it is fair to say that sustainability in its broadest definition is on the business agenda of many companies worldwide, many of whom have made conscious decisions to not only improve their financial performance, but also to optimize the ecological and social impacts of their operations.

The research question

The question that guides this book grew out of a study that we conducted during 2009 to assess the impact of a New Zealand wool yarn manufacturing company (WYM)[1] on the natural environment. WYM occupies a position as a premium yarn supplier to major carpet manufacturers in New Zealand, Australia, the USA and Europe, who operate mainly in the corporate carpet market. Knowing of our research interest in business sustainability, John,[2] an owner-director of WYM, invited us to assess the ecological impact of their operations. As a starting point we used *life cycle assessment* (LCA), an established tool used to assess ecological impacts associated with all stages of a product's life (Baumann and Tillman, 2004).

The genesis of this book was triggered when, part way through what was a relatively simple LCA, John asked two questions:

"What are we going to do with it when you finish?"
"How can we learn from it and make the business better than it is?"

When we looked at the underlying logic of these questions, John laid out an issue he felt was common amongst industrialists. He observed that much of the analysis done in the name of ecological sustainability 'stops' at the point when an LCA report or something similar is produced. John further observed that what commonly follows after an LCA is often 'greenwash'; that is public relations releases or marketing efforts that are deceptively used to promote the perception that a company's policies or products have a lower ecological impact than is actually the case (Strasser, 2011). Taking a more constructive approach, John viewed the LCA as having the potential to start a much grander project, one in which the assessment fed into decisions around a new strategy for WYM and ultimately the wool carpet industry. John also linked decision-making to the way that Paul (fellow owner-director) worked with their customers, creating new products not just in advance of their requirements, but also in response to them. Indeed, in the end, LCA has only a very minor influence on the present study, but it is important to note the contribution that it made as a foundation for this work.

Consequently, linking together organizational decision-making, new product development and business sustainability, in this book we ask:

"How do organizational decisions around new product development affect sustainable business outcomes?"

Theoretical foundation

In order to theoretically situate our work (Golden-Biddle and Locke, 2007, pp. 27, 31–37), we looked at the literatures on organizational decision-making, new product development and business sustainability. Individually, these literatures are huge; in combination they are overwhelming. In order to tightly constitute a theorized 'storyline' (Golden-Biddle and Locke, 2007, pp. 25–46), we carefully reviewed samples selected from each literature on the basis of frequent citation, the recommendation of academic colleagues and the journals in which they were published.[3] In so doing we followed best practice in undertaking a literature review. Where we perceived that a source demanded further analysis, we followed its citations back. What we were seeking was evidence of progressive coherence (Golden-Biddle and Locke, 2007, pp. 34–36) in the development of relevant concepts or evidence of the potential for constructing a coherent synthesis of thus far unrelated theories (Golden-Biddle and Locke, 2007, pp. 33–34), not to mention the 'space' in which we might make a theoretical contribution. It took a significant amount of effort and time to identify relevant theory and, eventually, a potential contribution. In the constraints of this monograph we do not attempt to detail the 'whole' of the literatures we utilized. Instead, we synthesize a coherent theoretical framework based on three narrow but highly cited and reputable communities of scholars. We now outline, to varying degrees the three main scholarly contributions that we exploit in this book.

A note for the reader is that the following paragraphs are imbalanced towards conceptualizing sustainability; this is because sustainability may be used in several contexts and is conceptualized in many different ways. In fact, we find that decision-making and strategic product creation feature much more heavily than 'sustainability' in the outcomes of our study, but, arguably, they are much more clearly defined in their literatures.

In terms of organizational decision-making, we elected to follow the influential body of the Carnegie School of organizational theory as an appropriate theoretical base (Cyert and March, 1992; March and Simon, 1993; Simon, 1997).

Theory on new product development (NPD) is large and widespread across many disciplines. Marketing is especially dominant in the development of NPD theory, but we sought a more managerial perspective (focusing on process more than product). Earlier work in decision-making (Smallman and Moore, 2010) supported by links drawn from the literature on the behavioural theory of the firm led us to the work of Sanchez (1995; Sanchez, 1996, 2002; Sanchez and Mahoney, 1996) on strategic product creation. What Sanchez (1995) describes as NPD is about incremental innovation, that is adapting existing techniques, technologies or materials to create product variants or synthesizing existing with new techniques, technologies or materials to create product variants (Ettlie, Bridges, and O'Keefe, 1984).

Theory around business sustainability in all of its forms is less coherent, because it falls into different or loosely related literatures focused on financial performance, corporate reputation and the ecological and social impacts of organizations. Clearly conceptualizing the latter two aspects of business sustainability is made more difficult because they are often mixed together. This is understandable given their origins in the concept of sustainable development, defined by the World Commission on Environment and Development (1987) as

> development that meets the needs of the present without compromising the ability of future generations to meet their own needs.

Hence, sustainable development contains within it two key concepts:

1   The concept of 'needs', in particular the essential needs of society, to which overriding priority should be given (social sustainability); and
2   The idea of limitations imposed by the state of technology and social organization on the ecological systems ability to meet present and future needs (ecological sustainability).

The theory on assuring financial sustainability of firms is well established in the accounting, economics and finance literatures (Tirole, 2006). In essence financial sustainability comes down to executive management finding the right balance of profitability, trading position (capital employed, revenue, stock, profit), liquidity, gearing (Luffman et al., 1991, pp. 76–92) and risk (Jorion, 2007).

Ecological sustainability in business, whilst heavily researched, does not yet enjoy an established academic consensus. Opinion is widely divided between those who dispute the basis of arguing for ecological sustainability – climate change denial (Lomborg, 2001) – and those who adopt a much more radical position – corporations are evil – (e.g., Welford). We adopt a more measured view, as advocated by (Dunphy et al., 2007, p. 52)

> we do not have to create a new political economy to achieve sustainability. It is enough to ensure that innovative environmental goods and services become a source of profit . . . market, government and NGOs all have a role

to play in industrial transformation incorporating more ecologically friendly principles.

Achieving this relies on organizations progressively adapting their value chain from conventional to ecologically sustainable production or service provision, evidenced in a range of quantitative measures and qualitative observations (Dunphy et al., 2007, p. 17).

As noted previously, social sustainability is often mixed in with ecological sustainability. Perhaps even more than the natural environment, the duty of businesses to be socially responsible is often the subject of passionate disagreement. However, in this work we adopt the approach of an authoritative scholar in the area who recently synthesized much of the literature (Banerjee, 2008), although even he is prone to mix together the social and ecological concepts:

> (1) corporations should think beyond making money and pay attention to social and environmental issues; (2) corporations should behave in an ethical manner and demonstrate the highest level of integrity and transparency in all their operations; (3) corporations should be involved with the community they operate in terms of enhancing social welfare and providing community support through philanthropy or other means.
>
> (Banerjee, 2008, p. 62)

There is a very limited literature that links decision-making with new product development (Ozer, 2005; Yahaya and Abu-Bakar, 2007). There is a more established body of knowledge around sustainable design (e.g., McDonough and Braungart (2002)), but not specifically sustainable product creation. We found no literature other than this that links across the three principle bodies of knowledge that we have explored.

Intended contribution

The literatures on organizational decision-making and strategic product creation evidence a progressively coherent understanding of the nature and process of these organizational activities. Our understanding of financial sustainability too demonstrates progressive coherence, although recent world events would suggest that the theory is *incommensurate* (in need of alternative ideas) – (Golden-Biddle and Locke, 2007, pp. 40–44). The knowledge of ecological and social sustainability is emergent; there are indicators of coherence around specific approaches. However, whilst this body of knowledge cannot be described as incoherent (Golden-Biddle and Locke, 2007, pp. 39–41), our understanding of ecological and social sustainability in a business setting is nowhere near as developed as that concerned with organizational decision-making, strategic product creation or financial sustainability; it is, arguably *incomplete* (Golden-Biddle and Locke, 2007, pp. 38–39). This offers a theoretical space to which we might contribute, but, research in ecological and social sustainability in organizations is common, and this is an increasingly crowded space. By contrast, the knowledge of the interrelationships between decision-making, strategic product creation and sustainability is sparse, perhaps even non-existent, since we found nothing of substance in the literature that links these three fields. Hence our contribution is to further develop our *inadequate* (Golden-Biddle and Locke, 2007, pp. 39–41) understanding of the relationships between organizational decision-making, strategic product creation and the three forms of business sustainability, by examining the links between concepts that characterize the three theoretical fields.

As we will show the theoretical gap that we address has two elements:

1 How decision-making processes affect strategic product development processes (e.g. the link between organizational learning and market research); and
2 How strategic product creation processes affect business sustainability outcomes (e.g. the link between speed to market and financial performance).

The case study

Selecting an empirical setting was primarily based on the requirement that it enabled the investigation of organizational decision-making processes within strategic product creation practices and their impact on sustainable business outcomes. Having done the LCA report for WYM we were familiar with the organization and its members were familiar with us. Having access of such quality is often difficult to achieve in organization studies. Hence, it seemed logical to extend our data collection and observations of the company to accommodate our enlarged interest in company processes, practices and outcomes. Hence, our fieldwork constitutes a single qualitative case study (Yin, 2011). We attended 175 meetings ranging from half an hour to over two hours in length and transcribed the recordings into 1,592 single spaced pages for further analysis. We also conducted secondary data collection supplemented with ten company documents and fourteen unstructured interviews.

Initially, thematic analysis using conventional coding techniques (Miles and Huberman, 1994) was conducted based on an analytical framework that reflected my theoretical synthesis. However, questions around the rigour and reliability of that coding led us to search for a more 'neutral' approach to coding, which we achieved through automated lexical analysis. The 'units' of analysis are strategic and operational episodes, evidenced in unstructured interviews, observations (of meetings and on the factory floor) and documents (Gioia and Chittipeddi, 1991; Hendry and Seidl, 2003, p. 180; Johnson, Langley, Melin, and Whittington, 2007, p. 58), that took place at WYM between April and October 2010. During that period, one of us was an embedded observer, physically located at WYM and working with John, Paul, their general manager George, their chairman, WYM's staff and some of their customers and suppliers. We were fortunate to have almost complete access to the firm at all levels and its records over the seven months of our fieldwork. We also had unlimited access to the whole factory and often did factory walks (daily and often more than once) observing and talking to the staff.

Furthermore, we benefited from interaction with the firm's business partners and customers.

Developing a single-case study was not simply a matter of convenience. Briefly, Yin (2009, pp. 47–50) identifies five rationales for undertaking a single-case design, where the case represents: the *critical* case in testing a well-formulated theory; an *extreme* or *unique* case; the *representative* or *typical* case; the *revelatory* case; or a *longitudinal* case. In this research, WYM was perceived to be a typical or representative case of a small and innovative company.

The book

Chapter 2 positions this research in relation to organizational decision-making processes and their impact upon conventional and sustainable strategy practices, product strategy practices, product creation practices, and ultimately business sustainability outcomes. It offers an overview of progressively coherent theories of organizational decision-making. The emerging theory of strategic product creation is subsequently detailed, before discussing emerging but still not greatly coherent theory around business sustainability aspects. We then offer a theoretical perspective around each combination of the primary literatures. Following this a theoretical synthesis is offered for understanding and investigating the research problem and research questions.

Chapter 3 provides an understanding of the research process we engaged in. Hence, we start by justifying our choice of research method. We then describe the research strategy followed by a presentation of the case study organization. A detailed approach to data collection then presented. Our initial approach to data analysis and the challenges presented to us at the time is then explained. These challenges led us to explore a different software tool and perform further analysis, which ensured rigour in our research study. The software that we utilized to perform the analysis of our data and the techniques employed during this phase are the presented.

Chapter 4 presents the findings based on the analysis of the data collected at WYM. We revisit our research questions and for each one present empirically derived concepts and justify them with a range of examples extracted from our data set. Hence the main findings for each research question are presented and the chapter then concludes with an identification of the main findings.

Chapter 5 creates the opportunity to bring together the fieldwork through the findings presented in chapter 4 with the three bodies of literature examined in chapter 2. In doing so this 'data-theory coupling' (Golden-Biddle and Locke, 2007, p. 52) looks into the forms and processes of organizational life encountered in the field. It also further evaluates the literature for similarities, differences or emerging patterns. Effectively it partly fills the research space for the study encountered in the writing, through joining the worlds of the field and academy with the aim to 'theorize . . . fragments of life' (Golden-Biddle and Locke, 2007, p. 53), shown through the numerous data excerpts. We revisit the empirical concepts presented in chapter 4 in order of strength (the ones that are referenced in most questions down to the ones that have fewer references). For each concept, we cross reference the relevant literature from chapter 2 and more to provide theoretical support for our empirical findings.

Chapter 6 ties together the books main findings and contributions and points to future research opportunities.

Notes

1 We have adopted a pseudonym for the company's name at the request of the company's directors. During the fieldwork WYM was the subject of an invited buy-out by a major carpet manufacturer. To identify WYM might cause commercial issues for both WYM and its new owners.
2 John and the names of WYM's senior teams are pseudonyms.
3 As much as possible we focused on 'tier one' journals such as *Administrative Science Quarterly*, the *Academy of Management Journal*, the *Academy of Management Review*, the *Strategic Management Journal*, *Organization Science*, the *Journal of Management Studies* and *Organization Studies*. However, we also extensively cite articles from a number of other established journals, notably: the *Journal of Cleaner Production* and the *Journal of Product Innovation Management*.

References

Banerjee, S. B. (2008). Corporate social responsibility: The good, the bad and the ugly. *Critical Sociology, 34*(1), 51–79. doi: 10.1177/0896920507084623.

Baumann, H., and Tillman, A.-M. (2004). *The hitch hiker's guide to LCA*. Studentlitteratur AB.

Caldwell, N., and Smallman, C. (1996). Greening the value chain: Operational issues faced by environmental management in the UK car manufacturing industry. *Eco-Management and Auditing, 3*(2), 82–90.

Costanza, R. (2000). Social goals and the valuation of ecosystem services. *Ecosystems, 3*(1), 4–10. doi: 10.1007/s100210000002.

Cyert, R. M., and March, J. G. (1992). *A behavioral theory of the firm*. New Jersey: Prentice-Hall Inc.

Dunphy, D., Griffiths, A., and Benn, S. (2007). *Organizational change for corporate sustainability: A guide for leaders and change agents of the future*. London: Routledge.

Ettlie, J. E., Bridges, W. P., and O'Keefe, R. D. (1984). Organization strategy and structural differences for radical versus incremental innovation. *Management Science, 30*(6), 682–695.

Gioia, D. A., and Chittipeddi, K. (1991). Sensemaking and sensegiving in strategic change initiation. *Strategic Management Journal, 12*(6), 433–448.

Golden-Biddle, K., and Locke, K. (2007). *Composing qualitative research* (2nd ed.). Thousand Oaks, CA: Sage.

Haropoulou, M., Smallman, C., and Radford, J. (2013). Supply chain management and the delivery of ecosystems services in manufacturing. In S. Wratten, H. Sandu, R. Cullen, and R. Costanza (Eds.), *Ecosystems services in agricultural and urban landscapes* (pp. 157–177). Chichester, UK: John Wiley & Sons.

Hendry, J., and Seidl, D. (2003). The structure and significance of strategic episodes: Social systems theory and the routine practices of strategic change. *Journal of Management Studies, 40*(1), 175–196. doi: 10.1111/1467–6486.00008.

Johnson, G., Langley, A., Melin, L., and Whittington, R. (2007). *Strategy as practice: Research directions and resources.* Cambridge, UK: Cambridge University Press.

Jorion, P. (2007). *Value at risk: The new benchmark for managing risk* (3rd ed.). McGraw-Hill.

Lomborg, B. (2001). *The skeptical environmentalist: Measuring the real state of the World.* Cambridge, UK: Cambridge University Press.

Luffman, G., Sanderson, S., Lea, E., and Kenny, B. (1991). *Business policy: An analytical introduction.* Oxford: Basil Blackwell Ltd.

March, J. G., and Simon, H. A. (1993). *Organisations* (2nd ed.). Cambridge, MA: Blackwell Publishers.

Matten, D., and Crane, A. (2005). Corporate citizenship: Toward an extended theoretical conceptualization. *The Academy of Management Review, 30*(1), 166–179.

McDonough, W., and Braungart, M. (2002). *Cradle to cradle.* San Francisco, CA: North Point Press.

Miles, M. B., and Huberman, A. M. (1994). *Qualitative data analysis.* Thousand Oaks, CA: Sage.

Ozer, M. (2005). Factors which influence decision making in new product evaluation. *European Journal of Operational Research, 163*(3), 784–801.

Porter, M. E. (1985). *Competitive advantage.* New York: The Free Press.

Sanchez, R. (1995). Strategic flexibility in product competition. *Strategic Management Journal,* 16, 135–159.

Sanchez, R. (1996). Strategic product creation: Managing new interactions of technology, markets, and organizations. *European Management Journal, 14*(2), 121–138. doi: 10.1016/0263–2373(95)00056–9.

Sanchez, R. (2002). Using modularity to manage the interactions of technical and industrial design. *Academic Review, 2*(1), 8–19.

Sanchez, R., and Mahoney, J. T. (1996). Modularity, flexibility, and knowledge management in product and organization design. *Strategic Management Journal, 17*(Winter Special Issue), 63.

Simon, H. A. (1997). *Administrative behaviour* (4th ed.). New York: The Free Press.

Smallman, C., and Moore, K. (2010). Process studies of tourists' decision-making: The riches beyond variance studies. *Annals of Tourism Research, 37*(2), 397–422.

Strasser, K. A. (2011). *Myths and realities of business. Environmentalism: Good works, good business or greenwash?.* Cheltenham, UK: Edward Elgar Publishing Limited.

Tirole, J. (2006). *The theory of corporate finance.* Princeton, NJ: Princeton University Press.

WCED. (1987). *Our common future.* Oxford: Oxford University Press.

Welford, R. (1996). *Corporate environmental management: Systems and strategies.* London: Earthscan.

Welford, R. (1997a). *Corporate environmental management: Culture and organizations.* London: Earthscan.

Welford, R. (1997b). *Hijacking environmentalism: Corporate responses to sustainable development.* London: Earthscan.

Welford, R. (2000). *Corporate environmental management: Towards sustainable development.* London: Earthscan.

Yahaya, S.-Y., and Abu-Bakar, N. (2007). New product development management issues and decision-making approaches. *Management Decision, 45*(7), 1123–1123. doi: 10.1108/00251740710773943.

Yin, R. K. (2009). *Case study research design and methods.* Thousand Oaks, CA: Sage.

Yin, R. K. (2011). *Qualitative research from start to finish.* New York: Guilford Press.

2 Theory in decision-making, new product development and sustainability

This chapter positions the book in relation to organizational decision-making processes and their impact upon conventional and sustainable strategy practices, product strategy practices, product creation practices and ultimately business sustainability outcomes.

Organizational decision-making

Narrowing the focus: choosing amongst six decision-making paradigms

The literature on organizational decision-making processes is extensive, with origins predating Simon (1997) *Administrative Behaviour: a study of decision-making processes in administrative organizations* which was originally published in 1947. Both Nutt (1976) and Smallman and Moore (2010) identify six paradigms in organizational decision-making theory, which align more or less.

The first paradigm is the classical concept of prescriptive, analytical or *bureaucratic decision-making* (Edwards, 1954; Fayol, 1949; von Neumann and Morgenstern, 1944; Weber, 1947), which claims that people collect and analyse information, eventually selecting an optimal solution from a range of alternatives. They do so by evaluating the advantages and disadvantages of each possible outcome and then choosing the one most appropriate to achieve their desired objective.

However, in its original formulation classical decision theory assumes 'pure' rationality. Prospect theory (Kahneman and Tversky, 1979) tackles this assumption in accommodating the notions of risk or uncertainty in decisions. This approach is also an example of what Nutt (1976), refers to as normative decision theory.

While this paradigm offers an apparent improvement over bureaucratic theory, it still fails to address the 'mediating processes that lead to a decision' (Decrop, 2006, p. 2). What Simon (1955) recognized in developing *behavioural decision theory* – the second paradigm – was that decision-making is bounded by limits on time, cognition and information. Bounded rationality (Cyert and March, 1992; March and Simon, 1958) takes the realistic view that individuals make decisions that are 'good enough' rather than optimal, based on the limits of the information and knowledge they have.

A variant of behavioural decision theory, is the third paradigm of *adaptive decision-making theory* (Payne, Bettman, and Johnson, 1993) that allows for natural dynamics in solving problems, finding that individuals use a variety of problem solving strategies, depending upon personal traits or characteristics, and problem and social contexts (i.e., bounds on their rationality).

Building out of adaptive decision-making theory, the fourth paradigm, *political or group decision-making* (Pettigrew, 1973) recognizes that most decisions are made in the context of groups (Delbecq, Van de Ven, and Gustafson, 1976). The model revolves around the resolution (or not) of tensions between groups through power relations and the resolution of conflict by consensus (Nutt, 1976).

The fifth paradigm offers a more pragmatic view of decision-making, which emerged shortly before the publication of Nutt's (1976) otherwise comprehensive review, which is the *garbage can* model (Cohen, March, and Olsen, 1972). The model does not conceptualize decision-making as a pattern of steps beginning with a problem and ending in a solution. Rather, independent streams of organizational events lead to outcomes or decision. The events may be problem 'points', potential solutions, opportunities for choice, or choices made by participants. These events are all mixed in the organizational 'garbage can'.

Also post-dating Nutt's (1976) work, but sharing many of the features of his 'open systems' model, is the emerging sixth paradigm of *naturalistic decision-making*. Most closely associated with Klein (1998; Lipshitz, Klein, and Carroll, 2006), this paradigm is commonly used in the study of real world decision-makers (Gore, Flin, Stanton, and Wong, 2015). The principal contribution that naturalistic decision-making makes is that it provides detailed descriptions of processes through which individuals or groups make decisions, and the contexts within which such decisions are made. Gore, Banks, Millward, and Kyriakidou (2006) note that this approach has yet to enjoy wider adoption in organizational decision-making research.

These six models offer a wide theoretical range from which to choose. Based on an extensive search of the literature, our choice among these models was guided by the 'strategy-as practice' movement, which is an increasingly influential body of knowledge focused on the practice of management (Golsorkhi, Rouleau, Seidl, and Vaara, 2010; Johnson, Langley, Melin, and Whittington, 2007). A particular focus of this movement is to better understand how strategic decisions are converted into action (Golsorkhi et al., 2010, pp. 12–14). Moreover, Johnson et al. (2007, pp. 18–19) aim to better understand the link between 'actors content activities' within organizations (e.g. relationship building) and 'actors process activities' (e.g. strategy debates) and identify significant opportunities for research in

> the interrelationship of the effect of organizational processes and systems on what people do, and vice versa, how people's activities affect organizational processes and systems, and, in turn, of the influence of these interrelationships on strategic outcomes.

Whilst our research is not principally concerned with strategy, we are interested in the conversion of decisions made by managers and directors into action. Reading around the abundant 'strategy-as-practice' literature, it became increasingly apparent that Johnson et al.'s (2007, pp. 37–38) logic indicated that behavioural decision theory (from the 'Carnegie' School) was an appropriate theoretical base (Cyert and March, 1992; March and Simon, 1993; Simon, 1997). This choice was reinforced as we considered the work of Van de Ven (2007, p. 203) in looking for guidance on how to design our research. Essentially, in addressing sustainability, WYM is seeking incremental and constructive (driven by aspiration rather than regulation) change. Based on Van de Ven's logic (Poole, Van de Ven, Dooley, and Holmes, 2000; Van de Ven, 2007, p. 203), a change such as this explicitly views organizational development as a process of formulation, implementation, evaluation and modification of goals based on what was learned or intended by an entity (Van de Ven, 2007, p. 203), that is the process is driven by an "envisioned end-state among individuals within the entity". For Poole et al. (2000), the authoritative theoretical frame for investigating such a process is also the Carnegie convention (March and Simon, 1993).

Hence, our decision-making focus is the Carnegie School of decision-making, originating in Cyert and March's *A Behavioural Theory of the Firm* (1992), originally published in 1963. This is supplemented by a brief discussion of a critique of research in the Carnegie tradition, which calls for a 'return' to some of the core strands of the original School.

The Carnegie paradigm: behavioural decision-making theory

Cyert and March (1992, pp. 161–176) conceptualize decision-making in the firm as a construct of four sub-processes as shown in Figure 2.1. What the Figure 2.1 illustrates is a weak representation of decision-making, even though it is based on rather more thoroughly conceptualized constructs. The issue is that neither the decision-making context (the environment) nor the behavioural outcomes of sub-processes are represented. The various steps of the sub-processes also mix decision 'gates' (questions the state of the environment or behavioural outcomes) with processes. This is typical of the issues presented by many authors in their attempts to represent complex organizational or management processes (Langley, Van de Ven, Smallman, and Tsoukas, 2013).

The sub-processes are described as:

1   *Quasi resolution of conflict*: most organizational theories assume that the coalition of people working for an organization is a coalition of members having different goals. Goals are viewed as a series of independent constraints imposed on the organization by its members. The conflict is resolved by using local rationality, acceptable level decision rules and sequential attention to goals (Cyert and March, 1992, pp. 164–166).

2   *Uncertainty avoidance*: uncertainty is a feature of organizational decision-making with which organizations must live. For example, in any business,

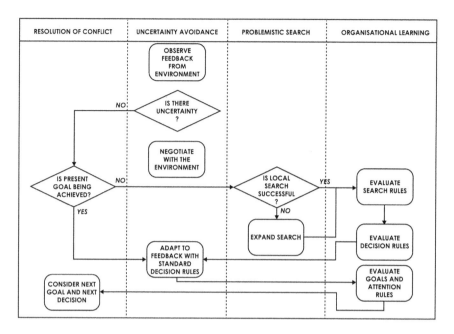

| RESOLUTION OF CONFLICT | UNCERTAINTY AVOIDANCE | PROBLEMISTIC SEARCH | ORGANISATIONAL LEARNING |

Figure 2.1 Carnegie decision-making process

there are uncertainties around the behaviour of the market, deliveries from suppliers, the behaviour and expectations of customers, the attitudes of shareholders, the behaviour of competitor firms, future actions of government agencies and so on. As a result, much of modern decision-making theory is concerned with the problems of decision-making under risks and uncertainty. The resulting solutions are mainly procedures for finding certainty equivalents or introducing rules for living with uncertainties. Studies indicate that firms achieve a manageable decision situation by avoiding planning that depends on predictions of uncertain future and emphasizing planning that is based on feedback decision procedures. Firms also make predictions about the behaviours of entities in their environment, especially competitors, suppliers, customers and other parts of the organization (Cyert and March, 1992).

3 *Problemistic search*: is search that is stimulated by a problem situation and is directed to finding a solution to this problem. Problemistic search is different to a search for understanding and is distinguished from random search that stems from curiosity. Problemistic search is usually motivated by a problem that generates a search with simple search rules that reflect simple concepts of causality. There is also bias in the search in the sense that there are different levels of training or experience in the organization, or different hopes and expectations, or communication bias that reflects unresolved conflict

within the organization. All of these influence outcomes (Cyert and March, 1992).

4   *Organizational learning:* organizations learn and exhibit adaptive behaviour over time (Argyris, 1982). Like individuals' adaptation to phenomena of the human physiology, organizational adaptation uses individual members of the organization as instruments. Organizations adapt with respect to three different phases of the decision process:

- *Adaptation of goals* – the goals with which we deal are in the form of aspirations and which have critical values that may change over time depending on experience.
- *Adaptation in attention rules* – just as organizations learn what to strive for in their environment, they also learn to attend to some parts of that environment and not to others. In doing so organization evaluate performance by explicit measurable criteria, which learn to attend while ignoring other, and organization learn to pay attention to some parts of their comparative environment and to ignore other parts.
- *Adaptation in search rules* – if we assume that the search is problem oriented we must also assume that the search rules do change. Thus the order in which various alternative solution to a problem are considered will change as the organization experiences success or failure with alternatives (Cyert and March, 1992, pp. 171–174).

The theoretical influence of the Carnegie paradigm

Argote and Greve (2007, p. 337) identify Cyert and March (1963) as "one of the most influential management books of all time", and one that provided the foundation for current research across the business disciplines as well as political science and sociology (Augier, Cohen, Dosi, and Levinthal, 2003; Augier and Kreiner, 2000; Augier and March, 2008; Augier and Prietula, 2007; Gavetti, Greve, Levinthal, and Ocasio, 2012; Germain and Cabantous, 2013; Luoma, 2016; O'Connor, 2013). Argote and Greve (2007, p. 337) find that Cyert and March's (1963) most particular influences are on current theories in organizational learning, and evolutionary economics. This apparently narrow influence is picked upon by Gavetti, Levinthal and Ocasio (2007) as a broad weakness in much of the theorizing that has taken place in the spirit of the wider Carnegie organization theory paradigm, but we shall return to this criticism later.

Argote and Greve (2007, p. 337) point out the paradox present in Cyert and March's (1963) chosen title, since the book neither offers a theory of the firm nor has inspired the generation of a singular theory. Simply, Cyert and March's (1963) model do not offer a "consistent set of defined concepts and assumptions, and derived casual predictions" (the definition of a theory given by Argote and Greve (2007, p. 337)). What has followed is many behavioural theories that have differing assumptions, and which offer differing predictions of behaviours. As Argote and Greve (2007, p. 337) note, those that have taken inspiration from *A Behavioural*

Theory of the Firm have often been selective in their choice of elements from the model, and understandably this has produced results that often look different from the original work's predictions. Gavetti et al. (2007) insist that this selectivity has ignored some of the key foundational elements of what is a much broader set of theoretical constructs and again, we will return to their critique shortly.

Argote and Greve (2007, pp. 337–338) argue that *A Behavioural Theory of the Firm* has offered to organization science a common outlook. Hence, whilst the theories derived from the original work are highly diverse, their common foundation has enabled a 'fruitful dialogue between perspectives', which in turn has enabled "the field of organization science to make rapid progress". Argote and Greve (2007, pp. 338–339) identify the common foundations not just with the elements of the model that We have previously outlined, but also with four commitments that they believe explicitly and implicitly underlie much of the research that *A Behavioural Theory of the Firm* has informed:

> 1. Focus on a small number of key economic decisions made by the firm. . . .
> 2. Develop process-oriented models of the firm. . . . 3. Link models of the firm as closely as possible to empirical observations. . . . 4. Develop a theory with generality beyond the specific firms studied.

The commitment to process-oriented models is, as Argote and Greve (2007, p. 338) point out, amongst the most widely adopted commitments and is an increasingly common research convention (Langley et al., 2013). However, as a random survey of any of the top tier management journals reveals, the effects of structures on organizational behaviour (often examined through quantitative analysis) remains the overwhelmingly dominant approach to advancing the knowledge of organization theory (Van de Ven, 2007, pp. 104–160). Argote and Greve (2007, p. 338) note that: "readers often examine the process explanation of a structural theory in order to judge its credibility".

The third commitment to empirical observation, discussed by Argote and Greve (2007, pp. 338–339) is highly relevant to this book. *A Behavioural Theory of the Firm* and research that has adopted a similar case study approach illustrates the considerable benefits that researchers gain from being 'close' to the phenomena that they are interested in. The key contribution is the clearly identified benefit of offering detailed or rich descriptions of events rather than summaries of them (Tsoukas and Chia, 2002).

Cyert and March's (1992) main contribution as identified by Argote and Greve (2007, p. 339) revolves around this commitment:

> theory should model organizational processes, and should be generated through systematic observation of processes in actual organizations.

Argote and Greve (2007, p. 339) raise the issue of the weaknesses in the quantitative work undertaken in *A Behavioural Theory of the Firm*. In essence, the propositions that Cyert and March (1963) developed were not rigorously tested, probably since the statistical techniques available to them were not sufficiently advanced to offer quantitative legitimacy to the theory. Subsequent developments in quantitative techniques and analysis have since taken up this challenge and have given the points made in *A Behavioural Theory of the Firm* more legitimacy.

Argote and Greve (2007, pp. 340–341) identify a wide range of influential organization and management theories inspired by *A Behavioural Theory of the Firm*. However, they further identify that Cyert and March's (1963) work as a major influence on the development of evolutionary economics (Nelson and Winter, 1982) and specifically organizational routines (Feldman, 2000; Feldman and Pentland, 2003). Argote and Greve (2007, pp. 341–342) also identify the influence of *A Behavioural Theory of the Firm* on organizational learning (typified in the work of Greve (2003)). Argote and Greve (2007, p. 344) conclude their review in identifying areas for further research, specifically

> a resurgence of interest in the internal structures and processes of organiza-
> tions . . . [and] a greater focus on understanding organizational decision-
> making . . . [requiring] theory that incorporates the social processes and
> contextual factors that affect organizational decisions . . . produce organiza-
> tional actions.

While Argote and Greve (2007) offer an apparently comprehensive review of *A Behavioural Theory of the Firm*, Gavetti et al. (2007) take a wider view of the Carnegie organizational research tradition. However, unlike Argote and Greve (2007) they consider that much of what has followed takes too narrow a perspective in focusing on organizational routines and organizational learning. They argue that researchers building on the Carnegie convention have progressively lost touch with "its defining commitment to a decision-centred view of organizations". They find that decision-making has given way to learning, routines and an overly focused perspective on change and adaptation. They further find that the organizational level of analysis has been largely replaced by a more micro or macro focus.

Where Argote and Greve (2007) majored on Cyert and March's (1963) four commitments, Gavetti et al. (2007) identify three foundational premises of the Carnegie School and out of these four theoretical 'pillars'. Of the foundational premises, the first is arguably the most important. In the Carnegie School organizations are distinct and peculiar social institutions. They are "shaped by, but not reducible to, human behaviours, social relations or market and nonmarket environments" (Gavetti et al., 2007, p. 525). For March and Simon (1993) what distinguishes organization from other social institutions is the coordination of individual and group action, the interaction between groups at different layers of organization and their interaction with the environment.

Second of the Carnegie School foundations is the dominance of decision-making in the School's view of organizations; that is decision-making is almost the singularly most important activity that takes place in an organization. This premise is common to all three of the books that marked the founding of the School.

Finally, and least clear, according to Gavetti et al. (2007, p. 526), of the foundational assumptions, is the School's belief in behavioural realism in its theory building. In the practice of research in the Carnegie convention this typically means the development of case studies or observations of people's behaviour in real-world organizations. Such observations lead to descriptive and properly contextualized analysis of organizations, usually supported by psychological, sociological or organizational theory. This is all aimed at developing rigorous (theoretical) explanations of organizational decisions, and the actions and outcomes that follow them.

From these three foundational premises, Gavetti et al. (2007, pp. 526–528) identify four theoretical pillars that focus on different aspects of complex organizational decision-making:

1   *Bounded rationality*. Based on his early work in applying psychology in economics Simon (1955) won the Nobel Prize in Economic Sciences in 1978. He successfully argued against neo-classical economics. He did not assume that people make perfectly rational choices and try to optimize economic outcomes. Instead, Simon argued that human rationality is constrained, not perfect, and that people seek satisfactory rather than ideal outcomes; that is, they 'satisfice'. Satisficing is a core concept throughout the foundational texts, and the use of bounded rationality in organizational theory is widespread.

2   *Specialized decision-making structures*. The Carnegie School also adopts the convention that "organizations are collective entities with some form of internal decision-making and communication structure" (Gavetti et al., 2007, p. 527). When the original Carnegie research was completed in the 1940s and '50s, most organizations had conventional hierarchical structures. This is reflected in the School's description of decision-making as occurring in distinct hierarchical levels with inputs and outputs to higher and lower levels informing the decision-making in those levels. This is a mechanistic picture, which does not sit well in modern organizations that are less hierarchical. Fortunately, this element of the Carnegie model gave way to a more fluid description of decision-making that focused more on process and the flow of decisions than the structure, leading to the garbage can model (Cohen et al., 1972).

3   *Conflicting interests and cooperation*. Of all of the 'pillars' identified by Gavetti et al. (2007), only this one explicitly ties to the decision-making model that is at the heart of *A Behavioural Theory of the Firm*. This is because it is a direct reflection of the quasi resolution of conflict process that is part of Cyert and March's (1963) decision-making model. Basically, the Carnegie School define an organization as "set of participants with conflicting interests, goals and knowledge [who] cooperate in collective action" (Gavetti et al., 2007, p. 527). This requires that organizations resolve conflict between individual parties, groups and coalitions through bargaining.

4   *Routines*. The Carnegie School is commonly associated with the notion that organizations are managed through routine-based behaviour. However, as Gavetti et al. (2007, pp. 526–527) indicate, the influential concept of organizational routines grew out of Nelson and Winter's (1982) reinterpretation of *A Behavioural Theory of the Firm* into evolutionary economics.

The originators of the Carnegie School do discuss standardised practices, programmes and operating procedures (routines) as central elements in organizational choice and search. However, routines are not a central concept in Carnegie theory. It is the later work of Nelson and Winter (1982) and their followers that has led to the dominance of research in organizational routines.

Of these four pillars, Gavetti et al. (2007, p. 528) argue that bounded rationality and routines have become highly influential in organization decision-making theory research and offer some suggestions on further development of this dominant paradigm. They suggest the need to reconceptualize bounded rationality, first by developing a better understanding of the impact of situational context on decision-making; implicitly arguing that the naturalistic decision-making paradigm (Gore et al., 2006) should be further developed in the context of organization studies. They also see the application of recent advances in social and cognitive psychology in furthering our understanding of bounded rationality, which might also be advanced by exploring the impact of organizational environments (Gavetti et al., 2007, p. 532).

Returning to their argument that individuals operate in decision-making structures, Gavetti et al. (2007, p. 532) argue for "renewed attention to the consequences of structure on organizational actions and outcomes". Gavetti et al. (2007, p. 532) also argue for a more sophisticated approach to understanding the role of agency and control in organizations. Instead of an individualistic model of agency, Gavetti et al. (2007, p. 532) suggest the adoption of Cyert and March's (1992) "view of the firm as a composition of political coalitions" as a means of representing 'real' organizational behaviours in organizational theories. Gavetti et al. (2007, pp. 532–533) adopt a complex systems perspective of organization, in which the organization adapts over time in response to organizational and institutional contexts. They suggest that this adaptation is affected by different types of decision-making structures. Overall, what Gavetti et al. (2007, p. 528) are looking for is a "behaviourally plausible, decision-centred perspective on organizations". This is in concert with the aims of our research.

As we detail in the next chapter, our dual analytical approach (conventional coding based on our reading of qualitative data, coupled with automated text analysis), requires the development of clearly defined key concepts. Hence following our discussion of the literature that we surveyed, we draw out and define what we judge to be the most relevant and important concepts in the literature.

Key concepts

In the case of decision-making, we define four key concepts upon which we base our analysis:

1   *Quasi resolution of conflict* comprises processes in which people cooperate to resolve conflict between themselves or others working inside or in association with an organization (Gavetti et al., 2007, p. 527).

2 *Uncertainty avoidance* refers to processes that help to progress decision-making under risk. This entails managing risk around five main issues: operational risks associated with the production and distribution of goods; strategic risks associated with competitive markets; legal or compliance risks associated with statutes, laws and regulation under which a firm operates; and financial risks associated with the financial operations of a firm (e.g. exchange rates, debtors, creditors) (Dowd, 1998).

3 *Problemistic search* is a process stimulated by a problem and is solution oriented.

4 *Organizational learning* refers to processes where firms learn through adaptation of goals (the quasi resolution of conflict), adaptation in attention (uncertainty avoidance) and adaptation in search (problemistic search).

Strategic product creation: dynamic resource management processes

Narrowing the focus: identifying coherent new product development theory

Similar to decision-making, the literature on NPD is large and spread across many disciplines. Marketing in particular has an extensive 'claim' to this phenomenon (Luchs and Swan, 2011; Swan and Luchs, 2011). However, we looked for a more managerially orientated perspective, especially one that might coherently link to the behavioural theory of the firm. The connection was not immediately obvious, but we found it as we reviewed a special issue of *Organization Science* edited by Argote and Greve (2007). In that issue, Pitelis (2007) makes a clear link between the behavioural theory of the firm and the theory of the growth of the firm (Penrose (1959) cited in Pitelis (2007)). Pitelis (2007) argues that the two theories have differences, but also similarities, and subsequently attempts to integrate important ideas from both theories. In the present thesis the most important elements of his synthesis (Pitelis, 2007, p. 483) are that:

- Firms are proactive learning organizations, operating under conditions of uncertainty and bounded rationality or imperfect knowledge.
- Intra-firm decision-making and resources are very important.
- A firm's internal resources do not often exactly match opportunities in the environment. This drives dynamic change in firms as they react to the external opportunities available to them (innovation).
- Organizational excess capacity or resources (known as slack) determine the structure, growth and performance of a firm.
- Consequently, slack may lead to problemistic search and may lead to innovation.

This seems to be a little way away from NPD, but, the link is made in Pitelis's (2007) connection between resources and innovation. We also identified a link to NPD in Pitelis's (2007, p. 478) own link from the theory of the growth of the firm to the resource-based view of the firm (Sirmon, Hitt, and Ireland, 2007; Wernerfelt, 1984) and then its extension in dynamic capabilities (Teece, Pisano, and Shuen, 1997).

The resource-based view (RBV (Sirmon et al., 2007, p. 273)) is based on the proposition that firms exist to create and maintain value, and that a firm's resources drive value creation through the development of competitive advantage. In this paradigm, the basis for competitive advantage is the possession of rare, valuable or inimitable resources, or resources that are not easily substituted. These resources must be exploited in order to create value. Sirmon et al. (2007, p. 273) argue that there is "minimal theory explaining 'how' managers [or] firms transform resources to create value" and that

> the RBV requires further elaboration to explain the link between the management of resources and the creation of value.

Sirmon et al. (2007, pp. 275–278) present "a dynamic resource management model of value creation" in an initial attempt to fill the theoretical gap that they identify. The processes that they identify in resource management (structuring, bundling and leveraging) are similar to Teece et al.'s (1997, p. 516) definition of dynamic capabilities as

> The firm's ability to integrate, build and reconfigure internal and external competences to address rapidly changing environments

In the dynamic capabilities paradigm, as indicated by Wang and Ahmed (2007, p. 41) a firm's ability to 'manage' its competences, as a set of distinctive and dynamic capabilities, enables it to survive, succeed and stand out from its competitors. Consequently

> the higher the dynamic capabilities a firm demonstrates, the more likely it is to build particular capabilities over time; the focus on developing particular capabilities is dictated by the firm's overall business strategy.

Hence, understanding the value of individual capabilities, as well as being able to communicate that understanding, enables firms to develop organizational skills that enhance the value of the firm (Sirmon et al., 2007, p. 285). Moreover, developing such understandings requires the development of "highly effective coordinating processes [that] facilitate the development of more creative and flexible capability configurations" (Sirmon et al. (2007, p. 285) citing Sanchez (1995)).

The RBV and dynamic capabilities theories deal with firm capabilities at the widest organizational level. In the present book, our interest is in specific capabilities focused on new product development, but that are also linked with strategic decision-making. Within the context of a large scale literature on strategic flexibility (Brozovic, 2018), Sanchez (1995) combines strategic flexibility and resource-based theories of the firm to explore dynamic product market competition. He develops a concept of strategic flexibility founded on: the flexibility of a firm's product creation resources termed as 'resource flexibility'; and "the coordination flexibility of the firm in using its available resources in product markets" (Sanchez, 1995, p. 135). Hence, as Sanchez (1995) explicitly derives his work from the RBV with an implicit link to the dynamic capabilities paradigm (Teece et al., 1997) (both works were published at around the same time and in the same journal), we elected to adopt Sanchez's work as the primary basis for our theoretical framing of NPD.

This aligns with later work, which finds that firms with high resource flexibility tend to foster radical innovation under high uncertainty by interacting with resource accumulation, rather than with resource acquisition. In contrast, firms with high coordination flexibility are likely to foster radical innovation under high uncertainty together with resource acquisition, rather than with resource accumulation (Li, Li, Wang, and Ma, 2017).

Strategic new product development

Sanchez (1995, p. 139) characterizes resource flexibility through three dimensions of resource 'use': the *range of alternative* uses for a resource (the greater the range the more flexible the resource is); *switching costs* from one use to another (the lower the cost of the resource the more flexible the resource is); and time required to *switch use* from one product to another (the shorter time to switch a resource the more flexible the resource is). It is the systematic interdependency of these characteristics that governs a firm's strategic flexibility.

Writing in 1995, Sanchez discusses the impact of 'new' technologies (e.g., computer-aided design and computer integrated manufacturing) on the flexibility of product creation resources, with concomitant innovations in management enabling new coordination flexibilities. The 'new' technologies are now commonplace, but his findings around product strategies, organizational forms and competitive logics that apply to dynamic product markets and remain relevant to the present book.

The new patterns of product competition in dynamic markets that Sanchez (1995, pp. 135–137) mentions (real-time market research, rapid product proliferation, intensive market segmentation, and rapid performance improvement) are realities of competition in present day firms, combining as they do technological and managerial innovations.

Sanchez's (1995, pp. 137–140) concept of strategic flexibility in product competition is a managerial response to uncertainty in dynamic product markets. The appropriate response is to formulate various strategic options for competing in such markets. These options jointly rely on resource flexibility as well as managerial flexibility. Hence, the flexibility of the firm is conceptualized in terms of achieving concurrent flexibilities in processes throughout the product supply chain. Of interest in the context of the present work is how organizations react to dynamic markets. Sanchez (1996, p. 124) highlights the relationships between a

Table 2.1 Strategic product creation concepts

Central strategy concepts	• Strategic flexibility • Fixed asset parsimony, leveraging of intellectual assets • Firm acts as 'network actuator' in developmental resource network • Coordination through modular product architectures • Flexible responses to changing market opportunities
Product strategy emphases	• Speed to market • Rapid performance upgrading through improved components • Proliferation of product variety, high model turnover • Flexible distribution networks
Product creation processes	• Real-time market research • Multiple short-term collaborations on electronically affected projects • Concurrent, autonomous, distributed developmental processes

dynamic product market context and central strategy concepts, product market emphases and the product creation process as outlined in Table 2.1.

Central strategy concepts

The central strategy concepts in the strategic product creation model centre around notions of: strategic flexibility, fixed-asset parsimony and the leveraging of intellectual assets, the firm behaving as a network actuator, coordination through modular product architecture and a flexible response to changing markets.

Sanchez (1996, p. 125) characterizes the *strategic flexibility* of a firm as the ability to respond quickly and advantageously to continuously changing market conditions. Hence following Sanchez's (1995) model, managers don't have to 'guess right' about future product preferences, instead they develop product ranges that more easily adapt to rapidly changing markets (Sanchez and Mahoney, 1996). As Sanchez (1996, p. 125) notes strategic flexibility is a characteristic of a firm that generates answers to potential future scenarios, looks at opportunities and manages uncertainty as best as possible. A firm that demonstrates strategic flexibility is able to reconfigure and redeploy its assets and its capabilities so that it can cope better with competitive market conditions (Sanchez, 1996, p. 125).

It is worth noting that James March has identified the need to understand the origin of preferences, their evolution, and to what extent they are a product of decisions made (Liu, Maslach, Desai, and Madsen, 2015, p. 151).

The concept of *fixed asset parsimony* is when firms choose to invest into building flexible intellectual assets like human capabilities and knowledge rather than acquiring and investing on inflexible or of specific-use assets (Sanchez, 1996, p. 125). This is linked to uncertainty about where technologies and market preferences are heading in the long-term as these sources cannot be determined with any level of precision.

No firm can identify or possess the entire range of assets that may be required to compete effectively in the future. Hence, firms begin to network with other firms to improve their abilities to assemble and delivering future new products (Sanchez and Mahoney, 1996, p. 125). In contrast to conventional notions of how firms can go about developing new products, these firms appear to function as *network actuators* and possess the following characteristics (Sanchez, 1996):

- they interpret real-time market data to identify opportunities for new products;
- they define modular product architectures for developing variations of new products;
- they establish 'just-in-time' relationships with suppliers of development, production, distribution and marketing capabilities; and
- they dynamically configure internal and external development, production, and delivery resources to create new product variations and rapidly upgrade existing models.

To enable the firm to be a network actuator requires that it adopts a *modular product architecture* philosophy. Modular product designs create flexible platforms for leveraging product variations and upgrades (Sirmon et al., 2007, p. 277). A modular architecture involves: (a) splitting the overall functionality of a product into its individual functions and components that support each function; and (b) standardizing component interfaces not allowing them to change during some period of time (Zellner, 2011).

Sanchez argues that modularity in product development practices achieves several forms of strategic flexibility: the ability to create greater product variety; the ability to upgrade products with improved components faster; greater speed to market, and lower design, production, distribution and service costs of products (Zellner, 2011, p. 614). Predicting future market responses to product variations is difficult. Creating modular product architectures relieves managers of the need to make risky guesses about future market preferences. Simply through specifying a statement of the range of market preferences that may need to be served in the future, enables product modularity to meet product attributes, performance levels and product costs a lot easier (Sanchez and Mahoney, 1996, p. 129).

Whilst much of the literature aligns to the view that modularity facilitates innovation, a few studies have revealed the downside of modularity. This is because in some cases it gives rise to inertia, which inhibits innovation beyond incremental change. The path to innovation or inertia is governed by the relation between managerial action, self-reinforcing mechanisms and characteristics of the environment (Gärtner and Schön, 2016).

Product strategy emphases

Product strategy in modular product architectures centres on the notions of speed to market, rapid performance upgrading through improved components, proliferation of product variety and flexible distribution networks.

Since development of components typically consumes the majority of time required for overall product development, concurrent development of components for a modular product design can significantly shorten total development times and improve the *speed* with which a firm can bring new products to *market* (Sanchez and Mahoney, 1996, p. 132).

New competitive product strategies based on *rapid performance improvement* become possible when a firm creates more robust modular product architecture. Such architectures accommodate a greater range of improved components and can quickly adopt improved or new components as soon as they become available from suppliers. Establishing a high rate of improved model introduction builds a progressive trend of heightened product performance. A trend such as this imposes higher costs and increases competitive pressures in the industry. When a firm adopts a robust modular design approach, it enables them to introduce improved models before imitators can bring their copies of current generation products to market (Sanchez and Mahoney, 1996, p. 128). Rapid performance improvement tests the capabilities of an organization to design, improve or upgrade components in their operations in a quick and orderly manner.

Modular product architecture permits changes in components that are within the range of variations allowed by its specified component interfaces. The ability to 'mix-and-match components enables leveraging of greater *product variety*, speeds the introduction of improved products and lowers overall design, production and other product costs' (Sanchez and Mahoney, 1996, p. 126). Firms that adopt modular product architectures develop what Sanchez terms as 'coordination flexibilities' (Sanchez, 1995, p. 139) to allow them to quick-connect with other firms so that they can develop, produce, distribute (*flexible distribution networks*) and market new products.

Product creation processes

Product creation processes are driven by *real-time market research* into evolving customer preferences for new products, facilitated by *multiple short or long term collaborations* with other firms, resulting in a *distributed development process*.

A firm uses *real-time market research* to learn more about market preferences, improve market knowledge and get feedback on consumer preferences (Sanchez, 1996, p. 130).

To obtain new or complement existing capabilities in product creation and acquire new market knowledge a firm may enter multiple long-term or short-term *collaborations* with other firms. This way the pressure put upon the firm for faster product development can be alleviated through the use of complimentary capabilities and expertise in product development, manufacturing distribution or marketing (Sanchez, 1996, p. 124). However, it is worth noting that while the effect of alliances such as these has been found to be broadly positive, the impact of alliance on strategic flexibility increases at a decreasing rate to a point, after which its impact turns negative (Dai, Goodale, Byun, and Ding, 2018).

In a modular product architecture, there is a decoupling of technology development and product development known as *distributed development process*. This strategy allows products to develop faster as the processes become concurrent, autonomous and distributed (Sanchez, 1995, 1996).

Key concepts

The key analytical concepts we have adopted are all defined in some detail in the preceding paragraphs. It is important to note that we only used some of the concepts defined previously and we explain why in the following paragraphs.

In the case of central strategy, we use three concepts; strategic flexibility, fixed asset parsimony and coordination through modular product architecture. We chose to omit the concepts firm as a network actuator and flexible response to changing markets. We revisit these two definitions and demonstrate the direct or indirect implication of elements from other concepts.

A *firm behaving as a network actuator* has the following characteristics:

- Interprets real-time market data to identify opportunities for new products (this is part of the real-time market research (RTMR) concept).
- Defines modular product architectures for developing variations of new products (this is an element of the coordination through modular product architecture (MPA) concept).
- Establishes 'just-in-time' relationships with suppliers of development, production, distribution and marketing capabilities (this is also element of MPA).
- Dynamically configure internal and external development, production and delivery resources to create new product variations and rapidly upgrade existing models (elements of speed to market (S2M), rapid performance upgrade through improved components (RPU) and proliferation of product variety (PPV) are all implied here).

The *flexible response to changing markets* is a characteristic of modular product architecture concept which provides managers with the flexibility to mobilize rapid responses to quickly changing market conditions. In addition, this concept implies elements of the *strategic flexibility* concept.

The remaining three central strategy concepts upon which we base our analysis are defined as follows:

1   *Strategic flexibility* is the ability of a firm to explore future scenarios, look at opportunities and respond quickly and advantageously to continuous change in competitive market conditions.
2   *Fixed asset parsimony* is when firms choose to invest into building flexible intellectual assets like human capabilities and knowledge.
3   *Modular product architecture* allows the decoupling of technology development and product development and enables firms to speed up product development by allowing processes to run concurrently and autonomously.

In the case of product strategy, we used three concepts: speed to market, rapid performance upgrade through improved components and proliferation of product variety. We chose to omit the concept of flexible distribution channels. This is because the strategic flexibility concept encapsulates the coordination flexibility of the firm in using its available resources in product markets (Sanchez, 1995, p. 135). Flexibility in distribution channels is what coordination flexibility of the firm achieves.

The remaining three product strategy concepts upon which we base our analysis are defined as follows:

1   *Speed to market* defines the speed with which a firm can bring new products to market.
2   *Rapid performance upgrade* tests the capabilities of a firm to design, improve or upgrade components in their operations in a quick and orderly manner.
3   *Proliferation of product variety* is the ability of a firm to develop greater product variety.

In the case of product creation, we used two concepts: *real-time market research* and *multiple short-term collaborations*. We omit the concept *distributed development process* as this is a premise encapsulated in the modular product architecture concept.

The remaining two product creation concepts upon which we base our analysis are defined as follows:

1   *Real-time market research* is a process where a firm learns more about market and consumer preferences via feedback and improves market knowledge.
2   *Multiple collaborations* enable firms to acquire complimentary capabilities and expertise from other firms.

Business sustainability

With theoretical framings of decision-making and new product development identified, the remaining major element odour theoretical framework relates to business sustainability outcomes, the foundations of which are in the concept of sustainable development.

The World Commission on Environment and Development (WCED) (1987) defines sustainable development as

> development that meets the needs of the present without compromising the ability of future generations to meet their own needs. It contains within it two key concepts: the concept of 'needs', in particular the essential needs of the world's poor, to which overriding priority should be given; and the idea of limitations imposed by the state of technology and social organization on the environment's ability to meet present and future needs.

Staib (2009, pp. 9–11) notes the response of business to the issues and risks associated with sustainable development has been patchy. Staib (2009, pp. 14–15) instead proposes the adoption of *environmental stewardship* as a part of business management, therefore emphasizing the need for businesses to

> be a part of the process of managing the environment for all people, for nature and the maintenance of its biodiversity and for future generations.

This captures the spirit of the WCED's definition of sustainability, and is aligned to wider thinking about stewardship models of management (Davis, Schoorman, and Donaldson, 1997), economics (Costanza, 2008) and sustainable supply chain management (Haropoulou, Smallman, and Radford, 2013). Staib (2009, p. 15) takes his ideas further, and in a direction that is relevant to the present study in also calling for *product stewardship*

> where business can be seen to have a role and responsibility for ensuring that the use of its products does not significantly impact the environment or the social and cultural aspects of communities.

However, in the wake of the recession of 2008 and the subsequent global financial crisis, Staib's (2009) position is not something on face value that businesses can easily accept. Many businesses are fighting for short-term survival, let alone sustainable growth. Consequently, most businesses have either gone backwards or failed to progress beyond standard accounting measures of environmental performance. Few have progressed beyond their 'fiduciary duty' (a legal or ethical relationship of confidence or trust regarding the management of money or property between two or more parties, in this case business managers and their investors) to true sustainability accounting and performance measurement (Cummings, 2009), although there are doubts about the effectiveness of such systems (Gray, 2010). It seems that only those major multinationals that are prone to causing environmental harm and are regularly under the public eye, put effort into this area of business reporting. There is also the question of businesses maintaining the duty of care that they owe to their employees.

However, the United Nations Environment Programme Finance Initiative (UNEP FI) and the World Business Council for Sustainable Development (WBCSD) (2010, p. 1) state:

> In the wake of the global financial crisis, business leaders and financial practitioners have been forced to rethink the fundamentals of mainstream asset pricing and business models. The crisis exposed the vulnerability of global capital markets and national economies to systemic shocks and the devastating effect these have on economic growth and stability.
>
> The exposure of markets to shocks has brought to light the importance of businesses and financial institutions incorporating systemic environmental,

social and governance (ESG) factors into fundamental financial analysis and business planning. The impact of climate change on the economic performance of businesses and nations is one such example and has been singled out by Sir Nicholas Stern as the single greatest market failure in human history. This has forced businesses and investors to rethink the basis for sustainable economic performance into the future.

UNEP FI and WBCSD (2010, p. 27) advise companies to

> Build knowledge and expertise on material ESG factors and sustainability in the context of their own companies and sectors . . . systematically integrate financially material ESG factors and sustainability into corporate decision-making and disclosure . . . [and] . . . communicate to investors the clear links between the management of financially material ESG factors and sustainability in the context of their own companies' strategy and in comparison to peer companies (i.e. within the sector).

They also advise the disclosure of quantitative environmental, social and governance (ESG) data and the development of a process for disclosing qualitative ESG data. Beyond companies they also offer advice to investors.

Whilst some authorities call for radical solutions to confronting and 'solving' corporate issues associated with sustainability (notably Welford (1997)), others adopt a more conciliatory approach; that is, they recognize that corporations, other large organizations and especially conventional small and medium-sized enterprises, tend to react adversely to radicalism. Taking a more pragmatic approach, most authorities, such as Stead and Stead (2004, pp. 55–121), instead position sustainable strategic management as an extension of conventional strategic management. Essentially they adopt a 'whole systems' view in which conventional strategy is set in the context of an ecological economic model rather than the narrower conventional economic model (Costanza, 2000). However, crucially, they also argue a strong moral case, where sustainable strategic management must be driven by people with strong ecological or social convictions.

What results from their approach is a 'closed-loop' value chain (Stead and Stead, 2004, pp. 83–84). This construct allows Stead and Stead (2004, pp. 104–121) to properly contextualize sustainable strategic management strategies, which range from functional level 'strategies' (more accurately these are tactics and include life cycle assessment, sustainability auditing and full cost accounting), through competitive level strategies (eco-efficiency and socio-efficiency) and corporate level strategies (confusingly again based on eco-efficiency and socio-efficiency), and finally to 'standing for sustainability' through 'triple bottom line' strategic thinking.

Marcus (2009) discusses how organizations may establish a strategic direction and then manage the firm whilst fulfilling their fiduciary duty and minimizing environmental or social harms. There is an expanding body of literature that finds that this is possible (Bansal and Hunter, 2003; Berry and Rondinelli, 1998;

Buysse and Verbeke, 2003; Dechant and Altman, 1994; Hart, 1995, 1997; Porter and Linde, 1995; Porter and Reinhardt, 2007; Porter and van der Linde, 1995; Priem, Rasheed, and Kotulic, 1995; Sharma and Vredenburg, 1998; Shrivastava, 1995a, 1995b).

Building on Hart's (1995) 'natural resource-based view of the firm', Marcus's (2009, pp. 39–40) approach links strategic capabilities with potential competitive advantage. The heart of his argument is to build values associated with environmental stewardship into the firm.

The adoption of a sustainable vision for a firm that is built on sustainability values and principles is primarily the responsibility of the firm's leaders. Effective leadership for sustainability (Benn and Dunphy, 2009, 2007) often involves considerable cultural change, but it is vital if sustainability is to become and remain established in any organization. Like so many forms of change, leadership for sustainability requires skills of diagnosis of areas requiring change and for implementation of changes, distributed across the firm's structure from the board through to operations. Only good implementation skills will help convince sceptical employees and carry those who are already environmentally committed. At the extreme a new system of corporate governance may be required to enable sustainability to take hold (Benn and Dunphy, 2007).

As we noted in the introduction to this thesis, sustainability in business is something that often leads to great debate. One of the most frequently cited arguments (from both 'sides' of the debate) is one put by the eminent economist Milton Friedman (1970) that "the social responsibility of business is to increase its profits". As noted by Dunphy et al. (2007, p. 8), neo-liberal economists use this as justification for privatization, focusing purely on shareholder returns and limiting the role of government in business, while their critics argue that this is destructive, endangering society and the natural environment. The debate between these two 'sides' has continued for forty years now, but most businesses recognize the need to balance their strict fiduciary duty with the need to look after their employees and other stakeholders in their businesses. Some also recognize the need to take care over their impact on the natural environment; in other words they strike a balance, and there is established empirical evidence of the value of this (Fombrun and Shanley, 1990). However, without maintaining commercial viability, firms cannot balance anything. Commercial viability is a prerequisite for assuring social responsibility and limiting environmental impact, and it is grounded in financial performance.

The individual literatures on decision-making, new product development and corporate sustainability are vast. However, they are dwarfed by the literature on corporate financial performance (Tirole, 2006). It is neither feasible nor appropriate for us to undertake a review of that literature. This is because we are focused on environmental, social and financial outcomes relating to the relationship between decision-making and new product development. Hence, we adopt what is generally recognized as the conventional view of financial viability within the strategy literature (Luffman, Sanderson, Lea, and Kenny, 1991, pp. 76–92), looking at financial viability, profitability, trading position, solvency and funding.

Key concepts

Sustainable businesses balance environmental and product stewardship with their fiduciary duty to their investors and the duty of care owed to their employees and operating under the overriding principle of *primum non nocere* ('first do no harm').

The business sustainability concepts we adopted in this book are tightly defined as follows:

1   *Environmental sustainability* in the production of goods or services entails a firm's minimization of energy consumption, natural resources usage and waste.
2   *Social sustainability* of a firm entails that their products or services do not significantly impact on the cultural aspects of communities and stakeholders or investors.
3   *Financial sustainability* of a business refers to a relationship of confidence or trust regarding the management of money between two or more parties – in this case business manager and their investors.

The preceding three sections deal with the principle elements of our theoretical framework, which we will outline shortly. However, before developing that synthesis, it is important to outline interdisciplinary contributions that lie at the boundaries of the three principle literatures. Hence in the next three sections We discuss literature that explores: decision-making in NPD; decision-making in sustainability; and sustainability and NPD.

Decision-making in new product development

Whilst not as extensive as some of the literatures We have dealt with previously in this chapter, there is an emerging body of research on decision-making in new product development (NPD). However, McNally and Schmidt (2011, p. 620) observe

> NPD and innovation decisions are strategic organizational decisions made by individuals or groups that affect firm performance. . . . Therefore, decision-making theories from organization theory, strategic management, psychology, and social psychology are relevant. Yet despite extensive theoretical decision-making research in these domains, there is a surprising lack of research examining NPD and innovation decisions from a theoretical perspective.

They then continue this line of argument citing, as we have, the considerable research opportunities in NPD decision-making following the neo-Carnegie convention, with its focus on organizational decision-making (Gavetti et al., 2007) rather than organizational learning (Argote and Greve, 2007). What our literature search revealed is a body of knowledge that is not yet coherent, although we have found sources that are relevant to our research interests.

Ozer (2005) notes the importance of new product development (NPD) for companies, but also notes that NPD is a risky and uncertain process. This, he points out, requires careful evaluation of new product proposals to improve the accuracy of decisions made around NPD.

Building upon a range of management theories and case studies, Ozer (2005, pp. 786–798) develops a framework that allows the analysis of contingencies in NPD in order to reduce negative impacts associated with decisions around new products. He identifies four major factors that need careful analysis: the nature of decisions; the type of individuals involved in decisions; the ways in which individual's opinions are elicited; and the way in which the opinions are aggregated.

In a wider empirical study, drawing on actual NPD issues in technology-based organizations Malaysia, Yahaya and Abu-Bakar (2007), identify four categories of NPD management issues: *strategic NPD management issues* (relating to the strategic objectives of the organization) that involve the use of "market knowledge, industry experience, organizational strategic objectives, as well as intuitive judgment"; *NPD project management issues* (relating to the administration of NPD project activities),which revolve around "business and product knowledge, project management experience, and risk-taking"; *process and structural NPD issues* (relating to the continuous effective operation of NPD activities), best met with the application of 'organizational learning and intuitive judgement'; and *people management NPD issues* (relating to the management of staff involved in an NPD project), which rely on the application of "managerial and supervisory skills . . . [and] . . . familiarity with organizational rules and norms".

Based on case studies of twenty-two business innovation projects in seventeen companies, Moenaert, Robben, Antioco, De Schamphelaere, and Roks (2010) identify the factors that influence strategic decision-making and their relative importance in the context of new product development. They find that decision-makers choices are determined by the assessment of "business opportunity . . . feasibility . . . competitiveness, and . . . leverage opportunities provided by the strategic option" (Moenaert et al., 2010, p. 840). A further on-site survey of 144 managers of a major chemicals company shows that "feasibility and business opportunity prevail over competitiveness and leverage at the decision-making moment". More detailed analysis reveals that the competitiveness of a strategic alternative is an important predictor of new project success. These contradictory findings at different levels of analysis demonstrate how complex decision-making is in NPD.

Earlier in this section we referenced McNally and Schmidt's (2011) concern that research on decision-making in NPD lacked a strong theoretical base, and that neo-Carnegie and the resource-based view might offer suitable theoretical frames for such work. Their comments were made in the context of editing a special issue of the *Journal of Product Innovation Management*. Most papers in the issue (De Clercq, Thongpapanl, and Dimov, 2011; Hammedi, van Riel, and Sasovova, 2011; Kester, Griffin, Hultink, and Lauche, 2011; Spanjol, Tam, Qualls, and Bohlmann, 2011) examine various decision points in NPD using a range of methods and different samples.

Spanjol et al. (2011) argue that it is commonly assumed that new product development teams make decisions based on executive goals and directives.

However, team members' individual motivational perspectives may also influence such decisions. Whilst the findings are limited by the nature of the sample (university students), Spanjol et al. (2011) find that when team members share the same motivational approach, executive goals and directive may be partly or completely ignored. Only where team members have differing motivations are NPD decisions consistent with executive goals and directives. Hence, whilst top management may apparently determine strategic direction for NPD, the influence that they exert on decisions relating to NPD may be diminished or eliminated where team members share similar motivations.

In looking at the management of a firm's product portfolio, Kester et al. (2011, p. 641) explore "decisions . . . about which projects to fund, to what levels, [and] at what point in time". Based on their grounded theory of product portfolio decision-making, they argue that

> portfolio decision-making may be better understood if it is considered as an integrated system of processes that considers these decisions simultaneously, along with other decisions such as those to continue a project with reduced funding.

More specifically, they find that effective NPD decision-making is grounded in three types of decision-making processes, based around evidence (product-related and market data), (managerial) power and (managerial) opinion. Kester et al. (2011) conclude that organizations' cultural factors (e.g., trust, ambition, leadership style) affect how these processes combine in overall decision-making process, and determine whether decision-making is rational and objective, or political and intuitive.

Hammedi et al. (2011) evaluate decision-making that takes place as products are conceptualized, that is the screening that precedes or halts initial development, which of course plays an important role in successful NPD. Because initial 'go/no-go' decisions on new product ideas are associated with high levels of uncertainty and ambiguity, Hammedi et al. (2011, p. 662) argue that it is important that the managerial and technical evaluation of such ideas is sufficiently flexible to enable the market potential of novel ideas to be fully realized. The counter-argument is that

> too rigorous a use of rigid evaluation criteria and inflexible methods have been shown to have an adverse effect on market performance of novel products.

They experiment with a model of how teams evaluate and discuss decision criteria, decision-support tools and working processes. Their results show that the effectiveness and efficiency of screening decision-making positively benefits from procedural rationality and transformational leadership. However, they also find that where a team over-analyses their criteria, tools and processes then this can undermine the benefits of rationality and leadership. They find that teams can improve their decision-making by more carefully and deliberately structuring their approach to decision-making.

De Clercq et al. (2011) explore the functionality of firms, looking at how organizational structure and culture enables collaboration across organizational functions and its impact on NPD. As well as evaluating the contribution of formal, structural factors (controlled by top management), they also analyse how less tangible factors enhance cross-functional collaboration to facilitate NPD. They find that cross-functional collaboration and product innovativeness are strengthened where decision-making autonomy and shared responsibility (both structural factors) are high. They also find that strong relational factors (e.g., social interaction, trust and goal congruence) have a positive effect on collaboration and product innovation. They conclude that

> organizations' relational context is more potent than their structural context for converting cross-functional collaboration into product innovativeness.
>
> (De Clercq et al., 2011, p. 680)

In developing research on strategic decision-making in NPD, Kandemir and Acur (2012) implicitly take up the challenge posed by McNally and Schmidt (2011). Combining theoretical perspectives on strategic decision-making flexibility in NPD (notably including Sanchez (1995)), the resource-based view of the firm (Sirmon et al., 2007) and dynamic capabilities (Wang and Ahmed, 2007), Kandemir and Acur (2012) find that the application of strategic flexibility in strategic decision-making for NPD activities is limited. They argue that this is strange given that such flexibility is widely accepted as a prerequisite for good corporate performance. They also find that it is difficult for firms to actively adopt strategic flexibility in decision-making, and that the relationship between "strategic decision-making flexibility and firms' resources and/or capabilities and success in the context of NPD" (Kandemir and Acur, 2012, p. 1), has not received a great deal of attention. Hence, their study attempts to prove how crucial strategic decision-making flexibility is in developing new products.

Based on data collected from a sample of 103 European firms, they find that the effects of long-term orientation, strategic planning, internal commitment, and innovative climate on proactive strategic decision-making flexibility are significant. More specifically, they identify the importance of 'champions' and 'gatekeepers', who through their clear understanding of their firm's resources and demand for their products can enhance decision-making in NPD and in NPD performance outcomes. In confirming Sanchez's (1995) theory, Kandemir and Acur (2012, p. 1) also find that strategic flexibility provides firms with an ability to adapt to changing environments and to create new market opportunities, product, and technological arenas, and to deliver successful new products.

Decision-making in sustainability

This section reviews the literature for evidence of decision-making for sustainable outcomes in business. This literature is challenging to deal with, because it is not concentrated in a specific discipline. We found few meaningful contributions that did not repeat what has been written previously. The ones we outline synthesize most of the key issues and theoretical arguments made.

Nilsson and Dalkmann (2001) employ a strategic environmental assessment (SEA) tool that integrates sustainability thinking into all stages of organizational decision-making process. To further enhance this integration Nilsson and Dalkmann (2001, p. 315) argue that there needs to be a clear understanding of each decision-making process so that environmental considerations can be improved. The way to achieve this lies in breaking each decision to a number of sub-decisions, 'incremental decisions' and linking them to the following SEA steps (Nilsson and Dalkmann, 2001, pp. 316–319):

1   *Environmental and social context*, which examines factors such as market trends and developments, previous issues and how they were resolved or the general political environment.
2   *Specifying the issue* once it has risen is an important step in determining who, what, where, when the issue will be dealt and resolved. In doing that the decision-maker will ground the problem and agree upon a 'workable resolution'.
3   *Goal setting* allows decision-makers to focus upon acceptable levels of achievement and consider a 'good enough' decision-outcome (satisficing).
4   *Information collection and processing* enables decision-makers to reduce complexity of the problem. However, the benefits of investing more time and money into acquiring more information are arguably diminishing as more information – leading to more time and money wasted – being collected.
5   *Alternative* decisions based on information collected and processed are developed. Nilsson and Dalkmann (2001) emphasize the importance of constructing alternative decisions that are robust, can be reversed if necessary and enable learning over time. A strategy of developing 'small steps', monitoring, reassessing and adjusting the situation according plays an important role in the development of alternative decisions.
6   *Evaluation, decision and implementation* steps follow a natural progression from the previous steps and assist further into turning a decision to a 'commitment of time, energy and resources'.

Waage (2007; Waage et al., 2005) argues that the various sustainability assessment tools have created more confusion than benefit. She recognizes that there are unanswered questions in product design around how best to integrate sustainability issues into decision-making processes. While acknowledging these challenges she offers a 'road map' that incorporates the standard product design process within the sustainability framework of ecological, social and financial outcomes. The road-map is built around four core phases:

1   *Understand and establish sustainability context*, which places the product development practices within the context of sustainability-aware product decisions. It enables decision-makers to better understand NPD processes considering sustainability factors.
2   *Explore and define sustainability issues*, which explores various product development concepts and considers the impact of each alternative concept on the ecological, social and economic aspects of sustainability.

3   *Define, refine and assess*, not only considers potential solutions emanating from phase 2, but also assess through tools such as LCAs the ecological, social and financial implications of the various alternatives so that the most desired approach good be implemented in phase four.
4   *Implement and receive feedback*, during which the product development team implements the desired solution and seeks criteria to monitor, evaluate and adapt product over time.

In their rather more comprehensive and properly grounded work, Benn and Dunphy (2007) cover the wider span of decision-making by tackling the issue of corporate governance and sustainability. At one point they specifically cover the issue of rethinking decision-making (Benn and Dunphy, 2007, pp. 27–28), focusing in on the importance of communication in decision-making concerning risk (for them risk is a foundational issue in sustainability). Their main argument is that decision-making for sustainability must include adaptive management techniques, which, by accommodating different stakeholder views, can offset the risks perceived by stakeholders. Interestingly, this reflects the view of James March himself that we need to better understand adaptive processes, including those through which we filter alternatives, and those by which new alternatives or options are generated (Liu et al., 2015, p. 151).

Hallstedt, Ny, Robèrt, and Broman (2010) explore a new approach to assess company decision systems regarding sustainability related communication and decision support between senior management and product development levels. They develop a theory based assessment approach and tested its applicability through action research in two small and medium-sized companies and two large companies. Their results are validated against the experiences of two management consultancies. Hallstedt et al. (2010) found that successful companies integrate sustainability into business goals and plans, backed up by suitable internal incentives and disincentives and decision support tools. Their study also found that their approach can be used as a template to assess the current state of sustainability integration in company decision systems.

Sustainability and new product development

Like decision-making for sustainability, sustainability and NPD cover many disparate disciplines. However, unlike decision-making for sustainability, the literature here offers more novel insights and contributions, demonstrates evidence of progressive coherence (Golden-Biddle and Locke, 2007) and seems to have a lengthier history, focused upon eco-design and life cycle assessment (LCA).

In terms of environmental product design, the most advanced firms have been found to demonstrate the following characteristics (Tukker, Haag, and Eder, 2000, p. 39):

* A clear management commitment to take sustainable development into account as an important factor in the company strategy.

- Product-related environmental activities are clearly embedded in a firm's procedures.
- The firm has experienced environmental staff with the knowledge and expertise to drive the company towards the green route.

In reframing product development, McDonough and Braungart (2002, pp. 15–16) see a world of abundance, not limits . . . offer[ing] a different vision. What if humans designed products and systems that celebrate an abundance of human creativity, culture, and productivity?

They question the fundamentals of design, using the *Titanic* as a metaphor for our industrial infrastructure (McDonough and Braungart, 2002, p. 17). They note that the Industrial Revolution was based on a vision of nature that is no longer accurate (McDonough and Braungart, 2002, pp. 18–26). They further find that the dominant industrial system and its variants are defined by a 'cradle-to-grave' production model (McDonough and Braungart, 2002, pp. 27–35), employing LCA (Heiskanen, 2002). The ISO (2006) standard describes LCA as

> a technique that addresses the environmental aspects and potential impacts such as use of resources and environmental consequences of releases throughout a product's life cycle from raw material acquisition through production, use, end of life treatment, recycling and final disposal.

Otherwise known as 'cradle to grave' assessment, LCA is a tool for environmental management and policy development. LCA evaluates all stages of a product's life from the perspective that they are interdependent, meaning that decisions made at one point along the life cycle may have consequences elsewhere (Curran, 2008, p. 2168). It is mainly used for comparing the environmental impacts of products rather than evaluation (Curran, 2008, p. 2168).

They also find gross domestic product (GDP) to be a perverse criterion of progress (McDonough and Braungart, 2002, pp. 36–37), which falls in line with ecological economic thinking (Costanza, 2008; Costanza, Hart, Posner, and Talberth, 2009). Their central argument is that we are producing unhealthy or crude products and that there is a need for a change in our approach (McDonough and Braungart, 2002, pp. 37–44). However, they do not support the contention of most environmentalists that we need to be 'less bad', that is the concept of 'eco-efficiency' as embraced by many corporations (McDonough and Braungart, 2002, pp. 45–67). Instead they call for eco-effectiveness (McDonough and Braungart, 2002, p. 78):

> the key is not to make human industries and systems smaller, as efficiency advocates propound, but to design them to get bigger and better in a way that replenishes, restores, and nourishes the rest of the world.

Baumann and Tillman (2004) demonstrate the importance of sustainable product development and how life cycle assessment may be used for greening product designs. Typically, product development is a multi-disciplinary activity involving people from different departments. The introduction of 'eco-design' in the product development phase is a challenge, requiring environmental consideration across the process by many different people (Baumann and Tillman, 2004, p. 236).

One of the important tasks during the product development phase is the development of design specification. This is a translation of customers' needs into precise, conformable details about what the product must do, without telling the product developers how to address it. Product development can also be described as several parallel processes and collaborations that handle and coordinate many issues, environment being one. Of course time pressure and trade-offs are characteristics of this process (Baumann and Tillman, 2004, p. 238).

Environmental considerations should start influencing the product development process as early as possible in the development phase. This is otherwise known as the eco-design phase where at one end of the spectrum we have the product improvement that refers to environmental improvement without changing the product technology (Baumann and Tillman, 2004, p. 239). On the other end of the spectrum we have the product redesign where parts of the product are developed further or replaced (i.e. design for recycling). However all these mentioned at present most practical efforts consist of incremental rather than radical changes while keeping the functionality of the product unchanged (Baumann and Tillman, 2004, p. 240).

As well as echoing the importance of many of the practices we highlight in strategic NPD (development speed, platform flexibility, outsourcing and offshoring, customer involvement and networks), and in directly citing McDonough and Braungart (2002), Eppinger (2011, p. 400) notes the 'fundamental challenge' posed by incorporating sustainability into design. He finds that the challenge is focused on four dimensions of materials used in product and process design:

1   The use of industrial materials that can be recycled into new industrial materials with no loss in performance.
2   The use of natural materials that can be fully reabsorbed into the natural ecosystem, creating new natural materials.
3   Not using or producing toxic or synthetic materials that cannot be safely processed in industrial or natural systems.
4   Restricting the use of fossil fuels in product design and development and promoting the use of renewable energy sources.

Following on from Eppinger (2011), in the same volume, Esslinger (2011) argues for the development of a 'sustainability-driven' business model. As is the case with Gibson (2006), in promoting this 'vision', Esslinger (2011), apparently ignores the whole literature on sustainability in management and organization studies. In essence his argument is for the stewardship model of business (Davis et al., 1997).

Perez-Valls, Cespedes-Lorente, and Moreno-Garcia (2015) identify green competences as dynamic capabilities based on green practices, routines and structures that can be used to detect opportunities, and to leverage them to transform organizations. They find that the impact of environmental best practices on performance is mediated by strategic flexibility. The further contend that such best practices are closely related to change and adaptation, because they target the prevention and management of environmental hazards. As such, environmental management and organizational flexibility are fundamentally connected. By their argument, a firm that has the capability to rapidly and effectively respond to environmental demands, will find it easier to transform environmental practices into cost saving and differentiation.

Business decisions, product development and sustainable outcomes: a synthesis

As indicated in the introduction, we aim to find links among three literatures. Each of the main literatures discussed earlier, decision-making, new product development and sustainability, individually demonstrate a 'progressive coherence' over time that is they largely

> "depict cumulative knowledge growth over time and consensus among researchers in a well-developed and focused line of enquiry".
>
> (Golden-Biddle and Locke, 2007, p. 34)

There are literatures at the margins of each of the main three, but the coverage is limited. This only partially filled gap means that an important perspective on business sustainability has been overlooked. An improved understanding and explanation of how decision-making affects product creation, product strategy, business strategy, decision-making, and the wider business sustainability seems highly relevant to the business discourse around sustainability.

Logically, decision-making processes must be the 'glue' that holds together product creation, product strategy and business strategy. If we are to have sustainable strategy, then the core outcomes of business sustainability must influence these three elements of organizational practice to begin to answer this, a model of what we term 'sustainable product development decisions' is offered in Figure 2.2, proposing links across the three main literatures and enabling the development of research questions.

In Figure 2.2, key concepts are grouped within their home literature 'strand'. However, in business reality, no concept, emphasis, process or outcome is easily separated from another. Also, these are proposed relationships, and there is no certainty that they exist. It is also important to stress the representation of time in all elements of the model, not least because our unit of analysis is time-bound. The concepts, emphases, processes and outcomes change and develop over time. We do not include any interdisciplinary constructs in this model. We argue that they would render it too complex. Instead we reserve them for consideration in the discussion of our findings.

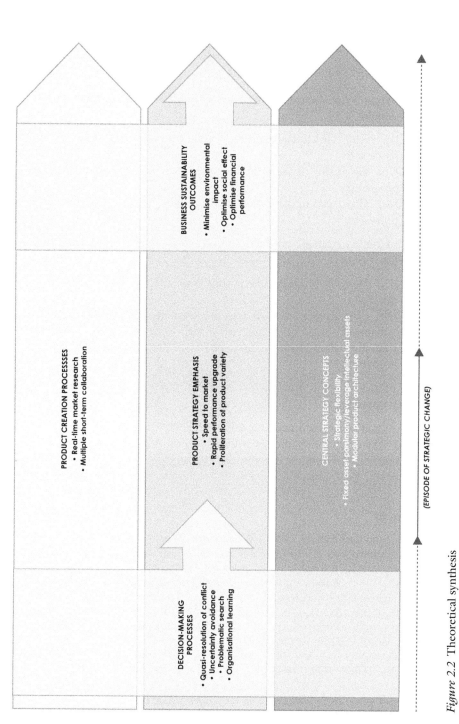

Figure 2.2 Theoretical synthesis

Research questions revisited

Based on the proposed model of sustainable product development decisions, we derived the following research questions:

> RQ1. How do decision-making processes affect strategic product creation processes?
>
>> RQ1a. How do decision-making processes affect product creation processes?
>>
>> RQ1b. How do decision-making processes affect product strategy processes?
>>
>> RQ1c. How do decision-making processes affect central strategy processes?
>
> RQ2. How do strategic product creation processes affect business sustainability outcomes?
>
>> RQ2a. How do product creation processes affect business sustainability outcomes?
>>
>> RQ2b. How does product strategy processes affect business sustainability outcomes?
>>
>> RQ2c. How does central strategy processes affect business sustainability outcomes?

Chapter summary

Based on a synthesized theoretical model, a series of research questions have been proposed. The model itself combines literatures on decision-making, strategic product creation and business sustainability outcomes.

In the next chapter, we provide a description of the research method we employed.

References

Argote, L., and Greve, H. R. (2007). A behavioral theory of the firm – 40 years and counting: Introduction and impact. *Organization Science, 18*(3), 337–349. doi: 10.1287/orsc.1070.0280.

Argyris, C. (1982). *Reasoning, learning and action: Individual and organisational.* San Francisco, CA: Jossey-Bass.

Augier, M., Cohen, M., Dosi, G., and Levinthal, D. (2003). Institutions and organizations: Introduction to the special issue in honor of James G. March. *Industrial and Corporate Change, 12*, 647–652.

Augier, M., and Kreiner, K. (2000). An interview with James G. March. *Journal of Management Inquiry, 9*, 284–297.

Augier, M., and March, J. G. (2008). A retrospective look at a behavioral theory of the firm. *Journal of Economic Behavior & Organization, 66*(1), 1–6.

Augier, M., and Prietula, M. (2007). Perspective-historical roots of the a behavioral theory of the firm model at GSIA. *Organization Science, 18*, 507–522.

Bansal, P., and Hunter, T. (2003). Strategic explanations for the early adoption of ISO 14001. *Journal of Business Ethics, 46*(3), 289–299.

Baumann, H., and Tillman, A.-M. (2004). *The Hitch hiker's guide to LCA.* Studentlitteratur AB.

Benn, S., and Dunphy, D. (2009). Leadership for sustainability. In R. Staib (Ed.), *Business management and environmental stewardship* (pp. 56–75). Basingstoke, UK: Palgrave MacMillan.

Benn, S., and Dunphy, D. (Eds.). (2007). *Corporate governance and sustainability.* London: Routledge.

Berry, M. A., and Rondinelli, D. A. (1998). Proactive corporate environmental management: A new industrial revolution. *Academy of Management Executive, 12*(2), 38–50.

Brozovic, D. (2018). Strategic flexibility: A review of the literature. *International Journal of Management Reviews, 20*(1), 3–31.

Buysse, K., and Verbeke, A. (2003). Proactive environmental strategies: A stakeholder management perspective. *Strategic Management Journal, 24*(5), 453–470.

Cohen, M. D., March, J. G., and Olsen, J. P. (1972). A garbage can model of organizational choice. *Administrative Science Quarterly, 17*(1), 1–25.

Costanza, R. (2000). Social goals and the valuation of ecosystem services. *Ecosystems, 3*(1), 4–10. doi: 10.1007/s100210000002.

Costanza, R. (2008). Stewardship for a "full" world. *Current History, 107*(705), 30.

Costanza, R., Hart, M., Posner, S., and Talberth, J. (2009). Beyond GDP: The need for new measures of progress. *The Pardee Papers.* Retrieved from www.bu.edu/pardee/files/documents/PP-004-GDP.pdf

Cummings, L. (2009). Sustainability accounting and reporting. In R. Staib (Ed.), *Business management and environmental stewardship* (pp. 226–252). Basingstoke, UK: Palgrave MacMillan.

Curran, M. A. (2008). Life-cycle assessment. In J. Sven Erik and F. Brian (Eds.), *Encyclopedia of ecology* (pp. 2168–2174). Oxford: Academic Press.

Cyert, R. M., and March, J. G. (1963). *A behavioral theory of the firm.* New Jersey: Prentice-Hall Inc.

Cyert, R. M., and March, J. G. (1992). *A behavioral theory of the firm.* New Jersey: Prentice-Hall Inc.

Dai, Y., Goodale, J. C., Byun, G., and Ding, F. (2018). Strategic flexibility in new high-technology ventures. *Journal of Management Studies, 55*(2), 265–294.

Davis, J. H., Schoorman, F. D., and Donaldson, L. (1997). Toward a stewardship theory of management. *Academy of Management Review, 22*(1), 20–47.

De Clercq, D., Thongpapanl, N., and Dimov, D. (2011). A closer look at cross-functional collaboration and product innovativeness: Contingency effects of structural and relational context. *Journal of Product Innovation Management, 28*(5), 680–697. doi: 10.1111/j.1540–5885.2011.00830.x.

Dechant, K., and Altman, B. (1994). Environmental leadership: From compliance to competitive advantage. *Academy of Management Executive, 8*(3), 7–27.

Decrop, A. (2006). *Vacation decision making.* Wallingford, UK: CABI.

Delbecq, A. L., Van de Ven, A. H., and Gustafson, D. H. (1976). Group techniques for program planning: A guide to nominal group and delphi processes. *The Journal of Applied Behavioral Science, 12*(4), 581. doi: 10.1177/002188637601200414.

Dowd, K. (1998). *Beyond value at risk. The new science of risk management.* Chichester: John Wiley & Sons.

Dunphy, D., Griffiths, A., and Benn, S. (2007). *Organizational change for corporate sustainability: A guide for leaders and change agents of the future.* New York: Routledge.

Edwards, W. (1954). The theory of decision making. *Psychological Bulletin, 51*(4), 380–417. doi: 10.1037/h0053870.

Eppinger, S. (2011). The fundamental challenge of product design. *Journal of Product Innovation Management, 28*(3), 399–400. doi: 10.1111/j.1540-5885.2011.00810.x.

Esslinger, H. (2011). Sustainable design: Beyond the innovation-driven business model. *Journal of Product Innovation Management, 28*(3), 401–404. doi: 10.1111/j.1540-5885.2011.00811.x.

Fayol, H. (1949). *General and industrial management.* London: Pitman.

Feldman, M. S. (2000). Organizational routines as a source of continuous change. *Organization Science, 11*(6), 611–629.

Feldman, M. S., and Pentland, B. T. (2003). Reconceptualizing organizational routines as a source of flexibility and change. *Administrative Science Quarterly, 48*(1), 94–118.

Fombrun, C., and Shanley, M. (1990). What's in a name? Reputation building and corporate strategy. *The Academy of Management Journal, 33*(2), 233–258.

Friedman, M. (1970). *The social responsibility of business is to increase its profits.* Retrieved from www.colorado.edu/studentgroups/libertarians/issues/friedman-soc-resp-business.html

Gärtner, C., and Schön, O. (2016). Modularizing business models: Between strategic flexibility and path dependence. *Journal of Strategy and Management, 9*(1), 39–57.

Gavetti, G., Greve, H. R., Levinthal, D. A., and Ocasio, W. (2012). The behavioral theory of the firm: Assessment and prospects. *Academy of Management Annals, 6,* 1–40.

Gavetti, G., Levinthal, D., and Ocasio, W. (2007). Neo-Carnegie: The Carnegie school's past, present, and reconstructing for the future. *Organization Science, 18*(3), 523–536.

Germain, O., and Cabantous, L. (2013). Introduction: Special symposium "Carnegie school and organization studies". *European Management Journal, 31,* 67–71.

Gibson, R. B. (2006). Beyond the pillars: Sustainability assessment as a framework for effective integration of social, economic and ecological considerations in significant decision-making. *Journal of Environmental Assessment Policy & Management, 8*(3), 259–280.

Golden-Biddle, K., and Locke, K. (2007). *Composing qualitative research.* Thousand Oaks, CA: Sage.

Golsorkhi, D., Rouleau, L., Seidl, D., and Vaara, E. (2010). *Strategy as practice.* Cambridge: Cambridge University Press.

Gore, J., Banks, A., Millward, L., and Kyriakidou, O. (2006). Naturalistic decision-making and organisations: Reviewing pragmatic science. *Organization Studies, 27*(7), 925–942.

Gore, J., Flin, R., Stanton, N., and Wong, B. L. W. (2015). Editorial: Applications for naturalistic decision-making. *Journal of Occupational and Organizational Psychology, 88,* 223–230.

Gray, R. (2010). Is accounting for sustainability actually accounting for sustainability . . . and how would we know? An exploration of narratives of organizations and the planet. *Accounting, Organizations and Society, 35*(1), 47–62.

Greve, H. R. (2003). *Organizational learning from performance feedback: A behavioral perspective on innovation and change.* Cambridge: Cambridge University Press.

Hallstedt, S., Ny, H., Robèrt, K.-H., and Broman, G. (2010). An approach to assessing sustainability integration in strategic decision systems for product development. *Journal of Cleaner Production, 18*(8), 703–712. doi: 10.1016/j.jclepro.2009.12.017.

Hammedi, W., van Riel, A. C. R., and Sasovova, Z. (2011). Antecedents and consequences of reflexivity in new product idea screening. *Journal of Product Innovation Management, 28*(5), 662–679. doi: 10.1111/j.1540–5885.2011.00831.x.

Haropoulou, M., Smallman, C., and Radford, J. (2013). Supply chain management and the delivery of ecosystems services in manufacturing. In S. Wratten, H. Sandu, R. Cullen, and R. Costanza (Eds.), *Ecosystems services in agricultural and urban landscapes* (pp. 157–177). Chichester, UK: John Wiley & Sons.

Hart, S. L. (1995). A natural resource based view of the firm. *Academy of Management Review, 20*(4), 986–1014.

Hart, S. L. (1997). Beyond greening: Strategies for a sustainable world. *Harvard Business Review, 75*(1), 67–76.

Heiskanen, E. (2002). The institutional logic of life cycle thinking. *Journal of Cleaner Production, 10*(5), 427–437. doi: 10.1016/s0959–6526(02)00014–8.

ISO. (2006). ISO 14040:2006, *Environmental management – Life Cycle Assessment – Principles and frameworks.* Geneva: International Standards Organisation.

Johnson, G., Langley, A., Melin, L., and Whittington, R. (2007). *Strategy as practice: Research directions and resources.* Cambridge: Cambridge University Press.

Kahneman, D., and Tversky, A. (1979). Prospect theory: An analysis of decision under risk. *Econometrica, 47*(2), 263–291.

Kandemir, D., and Acur, N. (2012). Examining proactive strategic decision-making flexibility in new product development. *Journal of Product Innovation Management,* n/a–n/a. doi: 10.1111/j.1540–5885.2012.00928.x.

Kester, L., Griffin, A., Hultink, E. J., and Lauche, K. (2011). Exploring portfolio decision-making processes*. *Journal of Product Innovation Management, 28*(5), 641–661. doi: 10.1111/j.1540–5885.2011.00832.x.

Klein, G. A. (1998). *Sources of power: How people make decisions.* Cambridge, MA: MIT Press.

Langley, A., Van de Ven, A. H., Smallman, C., and Tsoukas, H. (2013). Introduction to the special issue. *Academy of Management* (in press).

Li, Y., Li, P. P., Wang, H., and Ma, Y. (2017). How do resource structuring and strategic flexibility interact to shape radical innovation? *Journal of Product Innovation Management, 34*(4), 471–491.

Lipshitz, R., Klein, G., and Carroll, J. S. (2006). Introduction to the special issue. Naturalistic decision making and organisational decision-making: Exploring the intersections. *Organization Studies, 27*(7), 917–924.

Liu, C., Maslach, D., Desai, V., and Madsen, P. (2015). The first 50 years and the next 50 years of a behavioral theory of the firm: An interview with James G. March. *Journal of Management Inquiry, 24*(2), 149–155.

Love, K. D., and Roberts, K. J. (1997). Your company's identity crisis. *American Management Association Management Review* (October), 56–60.

Luchs, M., and Swan, K. S. (2011). Perspective: The emergence of product design as a field of marketing inquiry*. *Journal of Product Innovation Management, 28*(3), 327–345. doi: 10.1111/j.1540–5885.2011.00801.x.

Luffman, G., Sanderson, S., Lea, E., and Kenny, B. (1991). *Business policy: An analytical introduction*. Oxford: Basil Blackwell Ltd.

Luoma, J. (2016). Model-based organizational decision making: A behavioral lens. *European Journal of Operational Research, 249*(3), 816–826.

March, J. G., and Simon, H. A. (1958). *Organisations*. New York: Wiley.

March, J. G., and Simon, H. A. (1993). *Organisations* (2nd ed.). Cambridge, MA: Blackwell Publishers.

Marcus, A. A. (2009). Strategic direction and management. In R. Staib (Ed.), *Business management and environmental stewardship* (pp. 38–55). Basingstoke, UK: Palgrave MacMillan.

McDonough, W., and Braungart, M. (2002). *Cradle to cradle*. San Francisco, CA: North Point Press.

McNally, R. C., and Schmidt, J. B. (2011). From the special issue editors: An introduction to the special issue on decision making in new product development and innovation. *Journal of Product Innovation Management, 28*(5), 619–622. doi: 10.1111/j.1540–5885.2011.00843.x.

Moenaert, R. K., Robben, H., Antioco, M., De Schamphelaere, V., and Roks, E. (2010). Strategic innovation decisions: What you foresee is not what you get. *Journal of Product Innovation Management, 27*(6), 840–855. doi: 10.1111/j.1540–5885. 2010.00755.x.

Nelson, R. R., and Winter, S. G. (1982). *An evolutionary theory of economic change*. Cambridge, MA: The Belknap Press of Harvard University Press.

Nilsson, M., and Dalkmann, H. (2001). Decision making and strategic environmental assessment. *Journal of Environmental Assessment Policy and Management, 3*(3), 305–327.

Nutt, P. C. (1976). Models of decision making in organizations and some contextual variables which stipulate optimal use. *Academy of Management Review, 1*(2 (April 1976)), 84–98.

O'Connor, E. S. (2013). New contributions from old sources: Recovering Barnard's science and revitalizing the Carnegie School. *European Management Journal, 31*(1), 93–103.

Ozer, M. (2005). Factors which influence decision making in new product evaluation. *European Journal of Operational Research, 163*(3), 784–801.

Payne, J. W., Bettman, J. R., and Johnson, E. J. (1993). *The adaptive decision maker*. Cambridge: Cambridge University Press.

Penrose, E. (1959). *The theory of the growth of the firm*. New York: Wiley.

Perez-Valls, M., Cespedes-Lorente, J., and Moreno-Garcia, J. (2015). Green practices and organizational design as sources of strategic flexibility and performance. *Business Strategy and the Environment, 25*(8).

Pettigrew, A. (1973). *The politics of organizational decision making*. London: Tavistock.

Pitelis, C. N. (2007). A behavioral resource-based view of the firm: The synergy of cyert and march (1963) and penrose (1959). *Organization Science, 18*(3), 478–490.

Poole, M. S., Van de Ven, A. H., Dooley, K., and Holmes, M. E. (2000). *Organizational change and innovation processes*. New York: Oxford University Press.

Porter, M. E., and Linde, C. V. D. (1995). Towards a new conception of the environment-competitiveness relationship. *Journal of Economic Perspectives, 9*(4), 97–118.

Porter, M. E., and Reinhardt, F. L. (2007). A strategic approach to climate. *Harvard Business Review, 85*(10), 22–26.

Porter, M. E., and van der Linde, C. (1995). Green and competitive: Ending the stalemate. *Harvard Business Review* (September-October).

Priem, R. L., Rasheed, A. M. A., and Kotulic, A. G. (1995). Rationality in strategic decision-processes, environmental dynamism and firm performance. *Journal of Management, 21*(5), 913–929.

Sanchez, R. (1995). Strategic flexibility in product competition. *Strategic Management Journal (1986–1998), 16*(SPECIAL ISSUE), 135.

Sanchez, R. (1996). Strategic product creation: Managing new interactions of technology, markets, and organizations. *European Management Journal, 14*(2), 121–138. doi: 10.1016/0263-2373(95)00056-9.

Sanchez, R., and Mahoney, J. T. (1996). Modularity, flexibility, and knowledge management in product and organization design. *Strategic Management Journal, 17*(Winter Special Issue), 63.

Sharma, S., and Vredenburg, H. (1998). Proactive corporate environmental strategy and the development of competitively valuable organizational capabilities. *Strategic Management Journal, 19*(8), 729–753.

Shrivastava, P. (1995a). Ecocentric management for a risk society. *Academy of Management Review, 20*(1), 118–137.

Shrivastava, P. (1995b). Environmental technologies and competitive advantage. *Strategic Management Journal, 16*(5), 183–200.

Simon, H. A. (1955). A behavioral model of rational choice. *Quarterly Journal of Economics, 69*, 99–118.

Simon, H. A. (1997). *Administrative behaviour* (4th ed.). New York: The Free Press.

Sirmon, D. G., Hitt, M. A., and Ireland, D. R. (2007). Managing firm resources in dynamic environments to create value: Looking inside the black box. *Academy of Management Review, 32*(1), 273–292. doi: 10.5465/amr.2007.23466005.

Smallman, C., and Moore, K. (2010). Process studies of tourists' decision-making. *Annals of Tourism Research, 37*(2), 397–422.

Spanjol, J., Tam, L., Qualls, W. J., and Bohlmann, J. D. (2011). New product team decision making: Regulatory focus effects on number, type, and timing decisions*. *Journal of Product Innovation Management, 28*(5), 623–640. doi: 10.1111/j.1540-5885.2011.00833.x

Staib, R. (2009). *Business management and environmental stewardship*. Palgrave Macmillan.

Stead, W. E., and Stead, J. G. (2004). *Sustainable strategic management*. M.E.Sharpe.

Swan, K. S., and Luchs, M. (2011). From the special issue editors: Product design research and practice: Past, present and future. *Journal of Product Innovation Management, 28*(3), 321–326. doi: 10.1111/j.1540-5885.2011.00800.x.

Teece, D. J., Pisano, G., and Shuen, A. (1997). Dynamic capabilities and strategic management. *Strategic Management Journal, 18*(7), 509–533.

Tirole, J. (2006). *The theory of corporate finance*. Princeton, NJ: Princeton University Press.

Tsoukas, H., and Chia, R. (2002). On organizational becoming: Rethinking organizational change. *Organization Science, 13*(5), 567–582.

Tukker, A., Haag, E., and Eder, P. (2000). *Eco-design: European state of the art. Part I: Comparative analysis and conclusions*. Retrieved from Seville, Spain: http://ftp.jrc.es/EURdoc/eur19583en.pdf

United Nations Environment Programme Finance Initiative and the World Business Council for Sustainable Development. (2010). *Translating environmental,*

social and governance factors into sustainable business value: Key insights for companies and investors. Retrieved from Geneva: www.wbcsd.org/includes/getTarget.
asp?type=d&id=MzgzMDg

Van de Ven, A. H. (2007). *Engaged scholarship: A guide for organizational and social research*. New York: Oxford University Press.

von Neumann, J., and Morgenstern, O. (1944). *Theory of games and economic behavior*. Princeton: Princeton University Press.

Waage, S. A. (2007). Re-considering product design: A practical "road-map" for integration of sustainability issues. *Journal of Cleaner Production, 15*(7), 638–649.

Waage, S. A., Geiser, K., Irwin, F., Weissman, A. B., Bertolucci, M. D., Fisk, P., . . . McPherson, A. (2005). Fitting together the building blocks for sustainability: A revised model for integrating ecological, social, and financial factors into business decision-making. *Journal of Cleaner Production, 13*(12), 1145–1163.

Wang, C. L., and Ahmed, P. K. (2007). Dynamic capabilities: A review and research agenda. *International Journal of Management Reviews, 9*(1), 31–51. doi: 10.1111/j.1468–2370.2007.00201.x.

WCED. (1987). *Our common future*. Oxford: Oxford University Press.

Weber, M. (1947). *The theory of social and economic organisation*. Glencoe, IL: The Free Press.

Welford, R. (1997). *Hijacking environmentalism: Corporate responses to sustainable development*. London: Earthscan Publications.

Wernerfelt, B. (1984). A resource-based view of the firm. *Strategic Management Journal, 5*(2), 171–180.

Yahaya, S.-Y., and Abu-Bakar, N. (2007). New product development management issues and decision-making approaches. *Management Decision, 45*(7), 1123–1123. doi: 10.1108/00251740710773943.

Zellner, G. (2011). A structured evaluation of business process improvement approaches. *Business Process Management Journal, 17*(2), 203–237. doi: 10.1108/14637151111122329.

3 Methods for following the practice of small business management

The goal of this chapter is to provide an understanding of the research process we engaged in.

Hence, we start by justifying our choice of research method. We then describe the research strategy followed by a presentation of the case study organization. A detailed approach to data collection comes next. Our approach to data analysis is then explained. The software that we utilized to perform the analysis of our data and the techniques employed during this phase are then presented.

You can find full colour versions of each Figure at www.clivesmallman.com/decision-making-for-npd

Research method rationale

As noted in our literature review understanding decision-making as a process is amongst the most widely adopted Carnegie conventions (Argote and Greve, 2007, p. 338; Langley, Van de Ven, Smallman, and Tsoukas, 2013) as is the convention of empirical observation (Argote and Greve, 2007, pp. 338–339). Furthermore, *A Behavioural Theory of the Firm*, and research that has adopted a similar case study approach, illustrates the considerable benefits that researchers gain from being 'close' to the phenomena that they are interested in. The key contribution is the clearly identified benefit of gathering detailed or rich descriptions of events rather than summaries of them (Tsoukas and Chia, 2002).

Hence, we follow social constructionist conventions, gathering 'rich' information and perceptions about people through inductive, qualitative analysis based on discussions, participant observations, unstructured interviews, and document analysis. More specifically, this research adopts a single-case study approach as the specific inquiry method.

Research strategy

Building theories from case studies is a research strategy that involves using one or more cases to create theoretical constructs, propositions and theory from case-based, empirical evidence (Eisenhardt, 1989; Eisenhardt and Graebner, 2007). Case study research is the preferred inquiry method when examining contemporary events within a real-life context, where behaviours and issues cannot be manipulated (Yin, 2009, p. 11). Also, a case study approach is highly appropriate where research questions seek to explain 'how' or 'why' some social phenomena occur. This is because case studies deal with a wide variety of evidence (documents, artefacts, interviews and observations) beyond what might be available in a conventional historical study (Yin, 2009, p. 11).

A major reason for the popularity of theory building from case studies is that it combines rich qualitative evidence with mainstream deductive research (Eisenhardt and Graebner, 2007, p. 25). It is also fully aligned with research that follows the Carnegie tradition. However, even though theory building from cases is increasingly popular, it is not without its critics (Eisenhardt and Graebner, 2007, p. 26).

The foundation of all rigorous or credible empirical research is a strong grounding in the related literature. This enables the identification of a research gap, and facilitates the development of research questions that address such gaps. However, when building theory from case studies, researchers must take the additional step of justifying why the research question is better addressed by theory building rather than by theory testing. As a response to that challenge, the researcher must clarify why the research question has no existing theory that offers a feasible answer. Where research questions are driven by phenomena (i.e. 'why' questions), a researcher must frame the research in terms of the importance of the phenomenon and the lack of plausible existing theory (Golden-Biddle and Locke, 2007).

A significant challenge for researchers is choosing between the use of single or multiple cases (Siggelkow, 2007). While single case studies can richly describe the existence of a phenomenon (Siggelkow, 2007) multiple case studies provide a stronger base for theory building (Yin, 2009). While multiple cases are likely to result in better theory, theoretical sampling is more complicated. The decision to use multiple cases is based less on the uniqueness of a given case, and more on the contribution to the theory development within the set of cases. Hence, multiple cases are used to replicate or extend theory, or to eliminate alternative explanations (Yin, 2009); that is as a means of generalizing theoretical findings.

Siggelkow (2007) presents the persuasiveness of a single case with the 'talking pig' example and demonstrates how one powerful example can be very persuasive. Eisenhardt and Graebner (2007, p. 29) argue that in a single-case study, the challenge of presenting rich qualitative data is readily addressed by simply presenting a relatively complete rendering of the story within the text. To present a relatively complete narrative of each case in a multiple case scenario is impossible, as when a researcher tries to relate the narrative of each case to theory, then the theory becomes lost and the text 'balloons'. In a single case scenario though, the story is interspersed with quotations from key informants and other supporting evidence. The story is then intertwined with the theory to demonstrate the close connection between empirical evidence and emergent theory. This intertwining keeps both theory and evidence at the fore.

Yin (2009, pp. 47–50) identifies five rationales for undertaking a single-case design, where the case represents: the *critical* case in testing a well-formulated theory; an *extreme* or *unique* case: the *representative* or *typical* case; the *revelatory* case; or a *longitudinal* case. Yin (2009, p. 50) also distinguishes between holistic and embedded single-case design which turn on the unit or units of analysis involved.

In this research, we combine two of these rationales in a single holistic case study. The Wool Yarn Manufacturer (WYM) was perceived to be a typical or representative case of a small and innovative company, which was studied longitudinally.

The case study organization

The company started in 1992 in the hand knitted apparel industry. During 2000, when interest in hand knitted yarn slumped, demand shifted to carpet and rug yarn. The vision of the two founders, brothers Paul and John, was "to be the premium global manufacturer of custom engineered and exclusive fibre yarns for high-end carpet and rug manufacturers". This vision provided the basis for the company to grow considerably across the subsequent decade. WYM now manufactures high quality specialized wool yarn for domestic and international rug and carpet yarn manufacturers.

With the increase in production WYM moved premises to its present location with room to establish a facility capable of handling the large volumes required by customers and the diverse range of products the company now produces for top end carpet and rug makers globally. Within twenty years of its founding, the company has come a long way both on the local and the international scene. Over the past decade, the business has grown considerably developing on average about 45 tonnes of high quality specialized yarn a month that is mostly exported to many of the world's finest rug and carpet makers in Europe, US and the Australasia.

Paul's background in science and textiles gave the company a solid foundation for the hand knitted yarn industry. His expertise from being a member of the New Zealand Wool Board, and a miniature prototype of a specialty yarn production machine that he brought back home in his suitcase from England, coupled with his belief in the specialty yarn produced by the machine transformed the company to its current state. The product is a highly differentiated yarn that carries unique characteristics sought after by manufacturers of high quality carpets and rugs.

The company is now renowned internationally as a leader in specialty yarn technology, with a focus on producing products that are varied, technically demanding, well styled and difficult for competitors to copy, with a very low environmental impact. This mentality is reflected in all parts of the business from technically sophisticated enthusiastic staff, to market identification and distinctive branding. WYM's reputation as an innovator in technological and sustainable development has been recognized by winning the yarn innovation award at an international floor covering fair as well as an award for excellence and innovation in energy efficiency and renewable energy.

WYM core competencies

One of its core competencies is the ability to earn the trust of customers and become part of their development team. The WYM vision statement clearly indicates the need to

> Establish long-term relationships with both suppliers and customers

To date WYM is a supplier of choice to 80 per cent of their customers and is recognized as a world leader in specialty yarn technologies. Under the direction of the two brothers, WYM has grown to thirty-five employees over the last nineteen years, many of whom have enjoyed service with the company for over five years. Most of the staff has extensive experience in the textile industry. Plant configuration includes a carding machine with opening wool blend equipment, two gilling machines, six roving frames that put a distinct twist to the yarn, three production machines, a batch dryer, yarn winders and associated ancillary equipment. Sample dying facility to a 10kg capacity is also available.

The production capacity hit a low during the 2009 recession but picked up slowly after that. Despite other companies reducing their research and development budget during recession, WYM kept on experimenting with new product developments and maintained good relationships with existing customers which eventually paid off with an increasing product mix of 40–45 tonnes a month.

WYM's yarns are done to customer specification (tex, blend, type, etc.) and range from heavy count carpet yarns (>20,000 tex) to fine count apparel yarns (<500 tex). All finished products are shipped to the customers on completion of the order. The company also stocks a small amount of 2500 tex and 3600 tex rugs to meet immediate supply demands. WYM can also develop products using specialty yarns like Merino, Angora, Mohair and other blends although the demand for the latter yarns is very small due to high price.

WYM combines company core competencies of specialized yarn development and technically demanding yarn processing skills with its unique management philosophy to keep customers informed and up to date on product developments. This is reflected in the following statement from the general manager:

> before we set any policy, before we spent any money, before we make any decisions, before we take any action before we even open our mouth we should ask ourselves: If we were the customer, what would we want to see happen? Then that is what we should do.

This management philosophy enables WYM's customers to enjoy ongoing competitive advantage in their respective markets.

Staff structure

The focus of the company is on producing products that are varied, technically demanding, well styled and difficult for competitors to copy. This mentality is reflected in all parts of the business from technically sophisticated enthusiastic staff, to market identification and distinctive branding. As part of this process the board of directors appointed a general manager to oversee the growth of all business operations and the future direction of the company. The general manager, brought with him ten years of previous experience at senior executive level and a strong background in primary industry production processing and operations management.

The management team is also represented by the production and operations manager, the product development expert and co-owner Paul and the administration manager, all bring strong knowledge and enthusiasm into the team. Among key staff it is important to note here the site engineer, who brings a strong engineering background and the scientific advisor who provides technical expertise.

A good management team is important for the success of the business, but without a skilled staff base that is highly competent and has a 'can do' attitude and enthusiasm, WYM would not reach the level of the company that it is today. Most staff have been with the company for over five years and have come from a textile processing background. Staff numbers have increased as sales have increased. The general approach of WYM towards staff is training to use best business practices, focus around health and safety, and improve quality and product knowledge.

To ensure best practices in product development, information is visually displayed in designated business areas. Each time an existing or new product is going through the factory, the visual monitoring board with all the important information on 'hints and tips' and 'how to run' the specific product is displayed for staff to familiarize themselves and achieve top quality product each time, every time.

The objectives for Health and Safety, Engineering and Quality, has been set with the focus on having clear well documented expectations that conform to benchmark standards (e.g., AS/NZS 4801, ISO 9000) or to internal standards. WYM sets behavioural expectations from staff towards the company's strategic goals and market position. Its integrity statement as stated in WYM's *Operations Manual*, reads as follows:

> The focus of all work carried out is to treat everyone with respect (customers, fellow employees, suppliers and other business stakeholders). This is achieved by accepting responsibility for tasks performed, ensuring the various processes are in control and meet product and best practices standards.

This statement is a prime example of the ethos and values that underpin the WYM culture, which is evident in the products, product support and market relationships. New staff undergo the staff induction programme intended to introduce new employees to the company culture, relevant policies and procedures involved in their specific role, appropriate tours to show local area health and safety measures, as well as the whole company.

Process flowchart

The processes that the wool undergoes to end up as finished specialty product (see Figure 3.1) are listed here together with a brief description of each process:

- Opening and blending of the wool – the wool bales that arrive at the factory are opened and the wool fibres are broken up. This mechanical process needs the appropriate moisture content of the fibre (the addition of water and water soluble oil assist this process) to break up the wool clumps and makes the fibres more manageable for the next process; carding.
- Carding – the wool fibres are aligned together so that they roughly parallel to each other to produce a wool sliver.
- Combing (if it is merino wool) – this process removes any remaining vegetable matter and short fibres.
- Gilling – a further step into making the wool sliver consistent and even.
- Roving – this process converts the wool sliver to a lightly spun yarn ready to be used for the production process.
- Specialty treatment and drying – the proprietary specialty treatment gives WYM's yarn its distinctive characteristics; the actual process is commercially sensitive and is not directly relevant to the objectives of this study. The yarn is dried to the desired 'regain' level (moisture content).

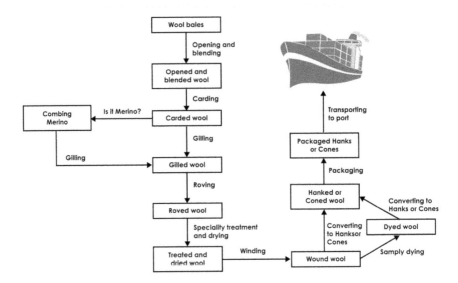

Figure 3.1 Life cycle for the production of specialty wool yarn at WYM

- Winding – the specialty yarn is wound on to cones or into hanks ready for packaging.
- Produce hanks – the specialty yarn is made into hanks (a specific length or weight of coiled yarn) and then dyed or packed.
- Sample dying – this process occurs only at customers request and it consists to no more than 3 per cent in weight of the finished product (i.e. specialty yarn).
- Packing the hanks or cones on pallets or in bales for shipping as they are in shipping container.
- Transporting to port.

Stage-gate product development approach

Product development at WYM plays an important role on future sales, maintains business cash flow and market position. Figure 3.2 demonstrates the stage-gate product development approach at WYM, with new products moving from the discovery – scoping – business case formation – development – and testing all the way to commercial launch stage only if appropriate commercial acumen and technical skills are applied at the various gates. Necessary 'must have' criteria at every gate must be met so that product development can proceed to the next stage.

Following the stage-gate approach, products progress from one stage to the next. After the discovery of new product ideas, gate one selects products that merit further work. Stage one will follow with a quick investigation of the product idea as well as project sculpting. Gate two questions whether the project warrants further work. If further work is warranted then stage two builds the business case by performing detailed investigation and project definition. Gate three checks if the business case can progress further into development. If the

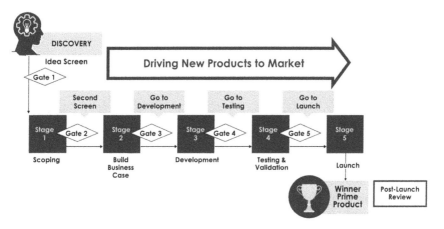

Figure 3.2 Stage-gate product development process

Source: Adapted from WYM product development manual

latter is true then stage three designs, develops and maps out the processing operations. Gate four investigates product testing options and progresses to stage four where prototyping, field trials and production rump-up take place. Finally, if the product is ready for launch then stage five does the full production and commercial product launch.

Data collection

Data collection set the boundaries for the study, collecting information through various sources: direct observations, interviews, participant observations, documentation, archival records and physical artefacts (Yin, 2009, p. 99). These major sources each provide advantages over others and no single one has a complete advantage over all the others. In fact, the various sources are highly complementary and a good case study will use as many sources as required.

In this research, we mainly employ direct observational data from meetings, although we also used documents and performed unstructured interviews to compliment the data collected. Data collected via interviews pose challenges such as impression management and retrospective sense-making (Eisenhardt and Graebner, 2007, p. 28). To mitigate this, the use of numerous and highly knowledgeable informants who view the focal phenomena from diverse perspective is often employed (Eisenhardt and Graebner, 2007, p. 28). Using multiple informants involves interviewing informants at different hierarchical levels, across different functional areas and experts outside organizations. Data collection using multiple informants substantiates the evidence gained from other sources (e.g. documents, observations, archival records), so helping to validate the data.

For this study, one of us was embedded in WYM for seven months. At the beginning of the data collection phase the observations consisted of several visits to WYM, to attend a meeting and then leaving. Soon it became apparent that more time was required to generate a rich data set, so we increased the number of meetings attended, the observations and the time spent in the work place. We collected as much data in as many diverse forms as possible. This approach is supported by King, Keohane, and Verba (1994, p. 24), who recognize it as an important guideline for improving data quality. Furthermore this offsets selection bias (Flick, 2007, p. 61; King et al., 1994, pp. 27–28). Another indicator of quality in this research was our extended participation – embedded for seven months from 9:00 am to 5:00 pm most weekdays and some Saturdays – which enabled us to have a long enough exposure to develop a well-founded understanding of the field and the issue under study.

There is always a risk of going 'native' when a researcher is embedded in the study field for prolonged periods of time. This was minimized by ensuring data triangulation and other techniques to assure reliability of the findings and analysis.

The field observations are categorized as *daily meetings* reporting on production and operational updates (116 transcribed documents), *weekly meetings* that cover a week's production run down and any major issues encountered (twenty-seven transcribed documents), monthly meetings around *quality* aspects of the company (nine transcribed documents) and *board meetings* where company strategy and other 'burning' issues were discussed (three transcribed documents), *ad hoc* meetings when external visitors arrived at WYM (twenty transcribed documents), *unstructured interviews* between the embedded researcher and staff members (fourteen transcribed documents) and finally *company documents* (eleven documents).

Most of the data we collected was through observing meetings without any participation. Marshall and Rossman (2006, p. 98) assert that observation entails the systematic noting and recording of events, behaviours and artefacts in the social setting chosen for the study. The observational record are referred to as field notes – detailed, non-judgmental, concrete descriptions of what has been said or observed. To capture the exact words in these meetings, we used a data-recording device. All the recorded meetings except one were transcribed verbatim immediately after the meeting ended. This was time consuming and on average one hour of recording would require three or more hours of transcribing. The detailed transcriptions sometimes required further clarifications. Hence, follow up questions were normally asked through email, phone or on person. The use of the recording device had its own challenges. For example, although it captured the exact words, it was impossible to determine the feelings of the participants or capture visual information particularly when discussing about production jobs around the board and using visual cues. Moreover, an additional challenge in transcribing was when people talk over each other during these meetings.

The data collection part of the study commenced culminated to a total of seven months' worth of data. During the first month, most of our activities revolved around observations to understand the new environment. To start we were unclear about the context of the various meetings, or their relevant importance. It soon became apparent that to get a full picture of the organization, we should aim to attend as many meetings as we could. After agreement with WYM's general manager, late in our first month, the embedded researcher was given a space in the front office of the factory and granted access to record the 'what', 'how', 'why', 'when', 'where', 'by whom' and so on, of company meetings, observations or informal chats with a recording device. As a result, the embedded researcher slowly gained access to the internal workings of the organization and got to know and be known by the other staff.

At the time of our fieldwork, WYM ran two eight-hour shifts: morning (6:00 am till 2:00 pm) and afternoon (2:00 pm till 10:00 pm). The embedded researcher had the opportunity to attend the day shift as most meetings run between 9:00 am and 5:00 pm each day.

For that data collection part of this research we employed several data sources. An important rule for any data collection is to report how data are created and how one came to possess them (King et al., 1994, p. 51). What follows is a breakdown of the various sources of evidence that we collected during the seven-month period.

Daily meetings

There were 116 daily meetings in total. Each took place at 9:00 am and lasted from as little as ten minutes to one hour or more. The meeting was chaired by the general manager and attended by the rest of the management team. The purpose of the meeting was to brief the attendees on the production status (the position of the various jobs in relation to the production schedule). The meeting was also a forum to report on operational issues from the previous day and to prioritize new customer orders onto the visual production planning board. Daily meetings were held in the 'war room' where the production planning board was located. As the factory ran from 6:00 am until 12:00 midnight each day, the daily meeting was a good vehicle for reporting on the production from the previous day.

Weekly meetings

There were twenty-seven weekly meetings in total. Each weekly meeting took place on a Tuesday at 10:30 am and lasted for a minimum of one hour. The meeting was chaired by the general manager, and attended by the rest of the management team, including the carding team leader.

At the start of the meeting the general manager worked with the carding team leader to agree the tonnage of raw wool sliver required to be carded in the following week, and to ensure that raw materials required were available or on order. Next, key performance indicators were presented to ensure that the business was on track and that there were no surprises. The indicators were:

- customer quality
- response time to customer
- forward orders
- production throughput
- dispatched
- production utilization.

Monthly meetings

There were two types of monthly meetings: the *quality meetings* (the embedded researcher attended nine in total) and the *board meetings* (we were given access to three).

The *quality meetings* took place during the first week of each month and were attended by the management team. This meeting was an important vehicle for any existing or surfacing production quality issues, the outcomes of which would form the base for the performance of the business and the six-monthly reports to the staff. The agenda of the meeting included the following key points:

1   Logged issues: the production manager reports on the most important internally logged issues – also referred to as 'managed' events – from the previous month. By doing so potential reoccurring issues were captured and analyzed further. If necessary – were the issue demanded further attention – an opportunity for improvement (OFI) record was created for that issue.

2   OFI monthly review reported and updated. The OFI register was updated and topics discussed. Hence, the meeting served as a vehicle to visit previous OFI records and update the staff on their progress. Each OFI was allocated a timeframe and assigned to a team member responsible for finding a resolution.

3   Quality systems progress reporting on various quality systems such as: the induction process and staff essentials manuals, or the product development flowchart.

4   Any important events raised and discussed and the meeting (i.e. the new production machine acquisition and installation, or the forthcoming merge with a major customer).

The *board meetings* were a monthly event. we had access to three board meetings in total. This was due to the sensitivity and the commercially confidential nature of some of those meetings.

The board meetings were attended by the general manager, the product development and sales manager and the two company directors. The general manager briefed the board on operational and other business issues since the last board meeting. He reported on the key performance indicators previously identified as well as happenings in areas of staff training, machinery upgrades or acquisitions (e.g., upgrade of the production machines), revenue and specialty yarn (in tonnes) information and trends on the business performance. Next, the product development/ sales manager gave an update on the sales position, market trends, potential new product developments, and ways of meeting customer demand. Finally, the company director who also held the position of accounting manager for WYM updates staff with the financial position of the company. If there was any sensitive information to be shared among the group – usually the case near the end of each board meeting – we were asked to leave the room.

Observations

The observations are collections of meetings that did not belong to any of the four categories (i.e. daily, weekly, board and quality meetings) identified previously. These meetings were either *unstructured interviews* or *ad hoc* meetings. The *unstructured interviews* represent informal conversations where no predetermined topic or questions were available. These interviews helped us to collect information using an informal 'chat' with staff members on various subjects ranging from employee perceptions on the company performance to specific individual challenges or aspirations. Although interviews of such nature make the development of comprehensive results more difficult, it can also reveal at times information that was not covered otherwise from previous collection methods. For example, we acquired knowledge on the steps involved in assessing the quality of the raw wool. The interviews mainly facilitated in obtaining answers on matters considered as 'jargon' or too technical for the embedded researcher. There were fourteen unstructured meetings in total.

The *ad hoc* meetings occurred when various visitors arrived at WYM without our prior knowledge. If meetings with visitors were not of a sensitive nature, we were asked to attend. Among the type of visitors that came through the front door at various points in time, we briefly mention people who did collaborative work with WYM like the engineering firm that installed a new production machine at WYM or a group of people – wool breeders – aiming to supply WYM with the raw material. There were twenty *ad hoc* meetings in total.

WYM company documents

In addition to the previous data collection methods, *company documents* were reviewed and analyzed. For case studies, the most important use of documents is to corroborate and augment evidence from other sources (Yin, 2009, p. 103). The documents hold evidence of production processes, operational issues, health and safety matters, induction training to new staff, managed events and quality events monitoring and best business practices followed. Some of them were complete, and some of them were in the process of been reviewed by WYM during this research. As part of the analysis we gathered and analyzed eleven substantive company documents:

- Product development manual
- Human resources manual
- Induction manual
- Operations manual
- Quality standards manual
- Health and safety intro
- Health and safety manual
- Health and safety procedures
- Environmental manual
- Production management
- Business plan

The documents were used in conjunction with data from the meetings.

Data analysis

We collected the data for this study over a sustained period of seven months in close proximity to the specific situation on *naturally occurring, ordinary events in natural settings* (Miles and Huberman, 1994, p. 10), which gave us a strong handle on the 'daily life' of WYM. Data collected in this manner makes them powerful for studying any process; we can go far beyond snapshots of 'what?' or 'how many?' and why things happen as they do and even access causality as it actually plays out in a particular setting (Miles and Huberman, 1994, p. 10).

However, there are challenges facing the researcher when compiling field data of this nature. The challenges are due to multiple data sources; some information comes from observations, some from interviews, other from structured ethnographic or elite sources, and other from archival records questionnaires, surveys, videos films etc. (Miles and Huberman, 1994, p. 55). There is often information overload and there is a 'golden mean' that every researcher has to find in their pursuit of data, which lies somewhere between recording everything versus recording too little (Yin, 2011, p. 156). In our case, there were certainly challenges due to the data overload – at least one meeting each day, sometimes two meetings or more. As each meeting was recorded via a data recorder the challenge was to transcribe it as soon as possible hence capturing the exact words and staying loyal to what was said (as far as possible). Due to the large number of meetings if not transcribed at the time, our job would be a lot harder, if impossible, later.

As is recommended in inductive case study research (Eisenhardt and Graebner, 2007; Yin, 2009) the starting point in data analysis is to establish an analytic strategy. One might start with a research question (Yin, 2009, p. 128) and "play" with the data as described by Miles and Huberman (1994), who suggest:

- putting information into arrays
- making a matrix of categories and placing the evidence within such categories
- creating data displays – flowcharts and graphics – for examining the data
- tabulating the frequency of different events
- examining the complexity of such tabulations and their relationships
- putting information in chronological order.

As a strategy in analyzing data we used the conceptual framework explained in literature review chapter and combined it with our research questions, which helped me generate selectivity.

Every case study has a 'story' to tell. This story is not a fictional account as it embraces real life data. Questions like: "what are the distinctive features of this study?", "how do the collected data relate to the research questions?" and or "have any new insights emerged?" (Yin, 2011, p. 183) were always in the researchers' minds throughout the entire analytic process. Rich familiarity with WYM was developed through synthesizing the data from the meetings, interviews and documents. The transcribed data amounted to 199 documents and totalled 1,592 single spaced pages collected over seven months. We divided all transcribed data among five folders (i.e. daily meetings, weekly meetings, monthly meetings, observations and finally WYM company documents). More orderly data enables strong analyses and ultimately more rigorous qualitative research (Yin, 2011, p. 182).

Leximancer text analytics software

In line with the recommendations of Rynes and Gephart (2009), the software tool we used is a computer-aided textual analysis tool, which allows a systematic, comprehensive and unbiased analysis of the data. Leximancer 4 is a text analytics tool which analyzes the contents of collections of textual documents and display the extracted information visually (Amaratunga, Baldry, and Sarshar, 2001, p. 4). The software serves as a data repository and organizes qualitative data systematically. It uses machine learning to automatically analyze and code text thereby largely removing the researcher's subjective views when interpreting data. The machine code that Leximancer executes conducts both conceptual analysis (concept discovery) and relational analysis (how concepts are interrelated).

Leximancer analysis runs through four distinct stages shown in Figure 3.3. Each stage executes in sequence, each completing a specific function in data analysis.

During the first stage – "Load Data" – we uploaded all documents that required further analysis. These consisted of 116 daily, twenty-seven weekly, eleven monthly and thirty-four *ad hoc* and interview transcribed meetings – a grand total of 188 transcriptions. The company documents (eleven documents) were not uploaded at the same time. Instead these were uploaded separately and analyzed with the same parameters. That allowed us to find similarities and differences in the way the business ran daily through meetings, versus what was documented.

The second stage "Generate Concept Seeds" is where Leximancer automatically identifies concept seeds by looking for words that most frequently appear in the text (Amaratunga et al., 2001, p. 11). They are referred to as seeds as they represent the starting point of the concept, with more terms being added to the definition through learning.

The user can run this stage using the default settings by clicking the "Generate Concept Seeds" button. Using the default mode termed as 'discovery' mode, the

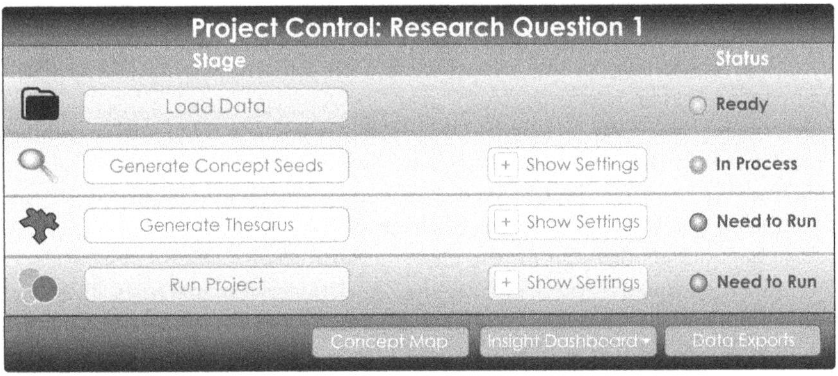

Figure 3.3 Four stages in Leximancer software

Leximancer software automatically discovers concepts without any user intervention. The 'discovery' mode will be examined later in this chapter. It is an important means of methodological translation.

Alternatively, this stage can be expanded to reveal two sub-stages within: Text Processing Settings and Concept Seeds Settings sub-stages. There are options to edit the Text Processing and Concept Seeds Settings. The Text Processing phase converts raw documents into the format used for processing. For example, the text processing phase (a) splits the information into sentences, paragraphs and documents, (b) removes weak semantic information (such as the words 'and' and 'of'), (c) identifies people, places or company names.

The Concept Seeds Settings phase is where the user can manually provide seed words. This is the path we chose to follow and it will be explained in more detail shortly.

Following on from the second stage the third stage "Generate Thesaurus" is where the user can interact with the seeds extracted automatically from the previous stage and edit, add or remove seeds from the list. This is important for a number of reasons (Amaratunga et al., 2001, p. 79):

- Automatically generated concepts may contain words that have similar meaning (such as think and thought) or other concepts that are not of interest to the user. In the Concept Editing interface provided at that stage the user can merge similar looking concepts into a single concept or delete concepts that she does not wish to explore further.
- The user may wish to create their own concepts. As previously stated this is the path we adopted in this research.

The final stage "Run Project" is where all Leximancer generated concepts as well as user-defined concepts are displayed under the "Concept Map" structure shown in Figure 3.4.

Concept Map

The Concept Map is a visual tool that provides a summary view of the material representing the main concepts contained within the text as well as information about how they are related. Essentially it allows the user to view conceptually a body of text as well as to perform a directed search of the documents. The interactive nature of the map permits the user to explore examples of concepts, their connections to other concepts as well as their links to the original text. In this way, Leximancer provides a means of quantifying and displaying the conceptual structure of the text and a means of using this information to explore interesting conceptual features.

The Concept Map is divided in two distinct sections: a visual display of concepts and their relationships to each other on the left and report tabs on the right for interacting with the map (Amaratunga et al., 2001, p. 13).

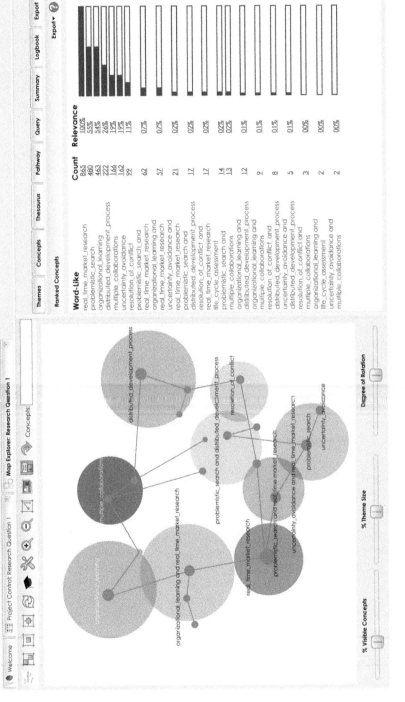

Figure 3.4 An example of a concept map and report tabs

Visual display

When the map first opens, only the top 50 per cent of the concepts[1] are visible on the map. These are the most frequently appearing in the text and the most connected (grey lines on the map) to the other concepts on the map. The user can alter the number of concepts appearing on the map (increase or reduce) by moving the *per cent Visible Concepts* slider at the bottom of the map. Increase the number of visible concepts by sliding it to the right and the opposite by sliding to the left. In this book, we use 100 per cent concept visibility. The lines connect concepts together on the map.

Figure 3.4 highlights basic Leximancer characteristics that merit further attention:

- The concepts are clustered into higher level *Themes*; these are shaded circles appearing on the map. Themes contain concepts that appear together often in the same pieces of text and hence tend to settle near one another in the map space. The themes are 'heat-mapped' to indicate importance. In Figure 3.5 the 'hottest' theme with the most textual hits is *real-time market research* near the top of Figure 3.5 and the 'coldest' theme is the *uncertainty avoidance and multiple collaborations* appearing in deep purple near the bottom of the. Similarly, to the concept visibility, the theme visibility can be altered through the *per cent Theme Size* slider at the bottom of the map. If the slider is moved to the right it makes fewer broader themes which embrace a larger number of concepts. By moving the slider to the left the themes become tighter.
- Concept frequency. The concept dots (i.e. the grey dots sitting behind concept names on the map) range in colour and in size from black to light grey. The darker and bigger the dot appears, the greater the number of text references coded at that concept (or compound). On this map, the concepts *real-time market research* and *organizational learning* are shown as the most frequent based on their shading and the size of the dot.
- Concept co-occurrence. This means that the same text reference is often coded in more than one concept. On this map, the concepts *real-time market research* and *organizational learning* appear very close to each other, indicating that the words that constitute them are often used together. If the text references for these two concepts are examined, we can see that 'information', 'understanding', 'knowledge' and 'learning' are terms frequently used in both concepts hence explaining their proximity. However, at other points *real-time market research* and *organizational learning* are used in conjunction with different terms, so they remain separate concepts.

In Figure 3.6, the theme *problemistic search* (the name of the theme takes its shading from the circle that it belongs to) contains concepts such as

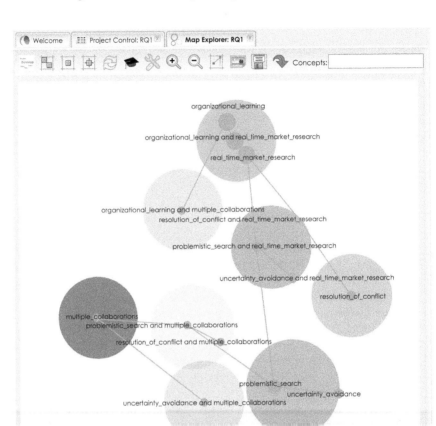

Figure 3.5 Concept map for RQ1

problemistic search and *uncertainty avoidance* which indicates that these concepts appear often together in the same pieces of text. Initially, each theme
takes its name from the most frequent and connected concept within that
circle. The user can always rename the theme.

The per cent theme size slider adjusts the size of the theme circles as the user
wishes. One can make all themes disappear by moving the slider to the left (0 per
cent) or make fewer themes by moving the slider to the right (100 per cent). In
the findings chapter, we use the Leximancer default theme size of 33 per cent.
The theme size slider simply changes the grouping of concepts on the map. If the
slider is moved to the right (increasing its value) it makes fewer, broader themes
that include more concepts. If the slider is moved to the left it makes narrower
themes with fewer concepts.

Figure 3.6 Themes for RQ1

Report tabs

The report tabs on the right section of the Concept Map (shown in Figure 3.7) enable the user to interact with the map and query the data. For example, the *Themes* tab displays all the themes according to the *per cent theme size* that the user chooses; each theme contains one or more concepts and takes its name from the most relevant concept within the theme. Additionally, the theme real-time market research takes its name from concept *real-time market research* which is the most relevant and connected concept within that theme with **841** text references.

The *Concepts* tab (see Figure 3.8) contains all the concepts that occur within the text. In Leximancer a concept is a collection of words that generally travel

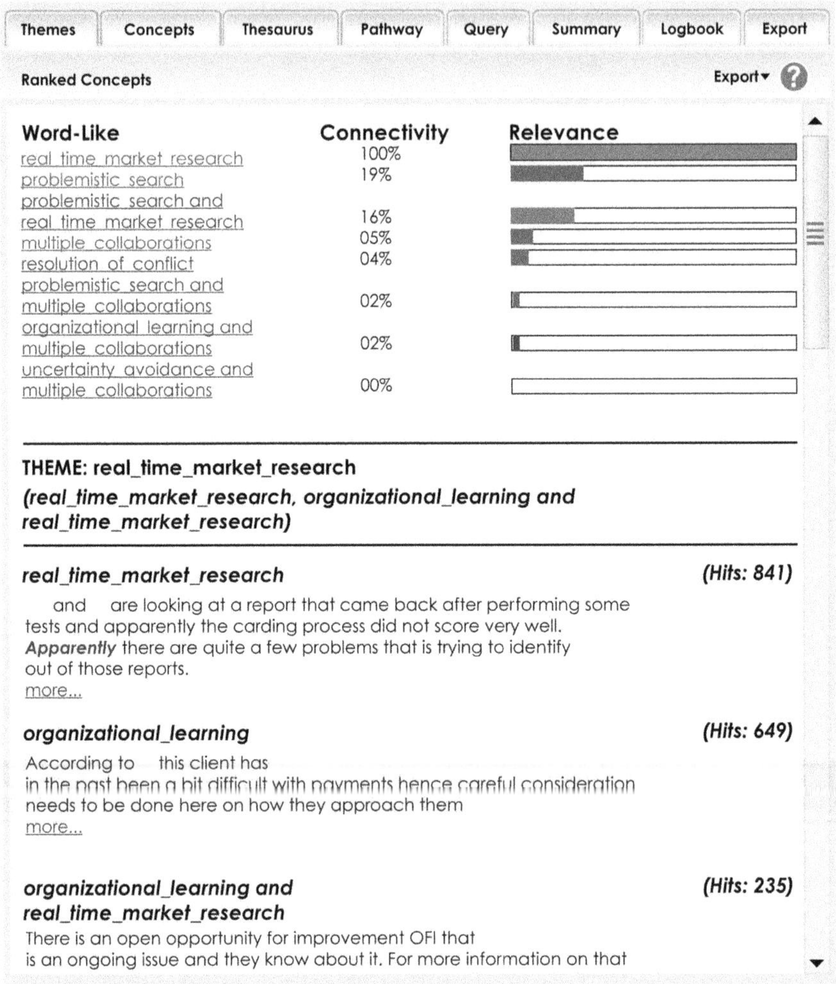

| Themes | Concepts | Thesaurus | Pathway | Query | Summary | Logbook | Export |

Ranked Concepts   Export▾ ❓

Word-Like	Connectivity	Relevance
real_time_market_research	100%	
problemistic_search	19%	
problemistic_search and real_time_market_research	16%	
multiple_collaborations	05%	
resolution_of_conflict	04%	
problemistic_search and multiple_collaborations	02%	
organizational_learning and multiple_collaborations	02%	
uncertainty_avoidance and multiple_collaborations	00%	

THEME: real_time_market_research
(real_time_market_research, organizational_learning and real_time_market_research)

---

real_time_market_research   *(Hits: 841)*

   and   are looking at a report that came back after performing some
tests and apparently the carding process did not score very well.
Apparently there are quite a few problems that is trying to identify
out of those reports.
more...

organizational_learning   *(Hits: 649)*

According to   this client has
in the past been a bit difficult with payments hence careful consideration
needs to be done here on how they approach them
more...

organizational_learning and   *(Hits: 235)*
real_time_market_research
There is an open opportunity for improvement OFI that
is an ongoing issue and they know about it. For more information on that

Figure 3.7 Themes tab

together throughout the text. For example, the concept *learning* may contain the words thinking, examine, observation, etc. These key words are weighted according to how frequently they occur in sentences containing the *learning* concept. Sentences are tagged as containing the concept if enough accumulated evidence of key words is found. In Leximancer, the definition of each concept (i.e. the set of weighted key words) is automatically learned from the text itself. Concepts are classified as name like when they refer to people names, places or companies and those appear in upper case first letter. All other concepts are classified as word-like concepts and appear in lower case on the map.

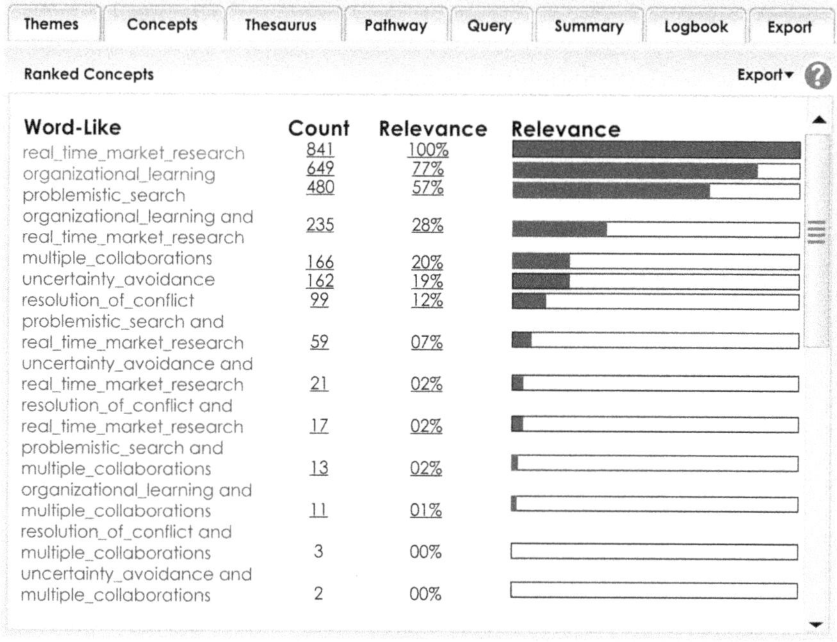

Figure 3.8 Concepts tab

The concepts we developed for this book are word-like concepts. No name-like concepts are included. Figure 3.8 displays all concepts the number of text references for each concept (Count) and the importance of each concept in relation to the other concepts (Relevance). The relevance is the importance of the concept in relation to the rest of the concepts. The highest count shows 100 per cent relevance, whilst the second highest count has for relevance the proportion of its count compared with the highest count. For example, in Figure 3.11, the concept *problemistic search* has a count of 480 text references and a relevance of 57 per cent, which is the proportion of its count to the highest count (480/841 = 0.57). If a concept or a compound concept has no text references, it is completely omitted from the concepts list.

The key words that define each concept, otherwise known as 'seed words', are constantly updated during the learning stage and eventually form the *'Thesaurus'* of words that define each concept. The *Thesaurus* tab (see Figure 3.9) contains each concept with each associated seed word and their weightings, which indicate the words' relative importance in the concept generation. In Figure 3.9 the concept *problemistic search* has seed words such as *problem, key, trouble* and others. The *Thesaurus* list also shows the relevancy weightings associated with each indicative word (Score). The iterations count (top left) tells the number of

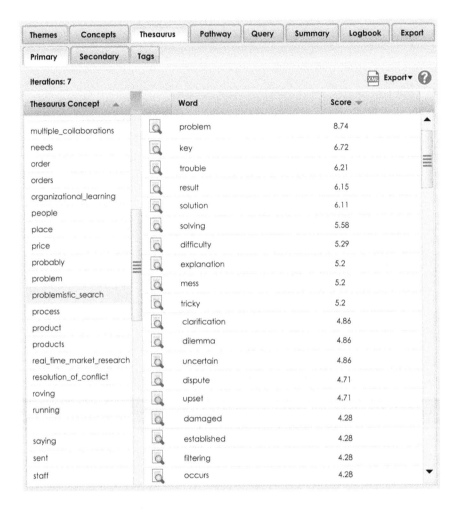

Figure 3.9 Thesaurus tab

times the corpus was reread and coded with evolving concept definitions before a stable classification result was achieved. In this example, the corpus was reread seven times.

The user can click on the Evidence button (the magnifying lens icon) to the left of the thesaurus item to browse the text excerpts for the concept of interest. This opens the *Query* tab which provides text references for the seed word *problem* within the *problemistic search* concept. Every reference is identified through the document file that it came from. The total number of references for word *problem* (279) is shown at the bottom right-hand corner (see Figure 3.10).

These are all the tabs we used in the current study. This interactive nature of the map elements helps the researcher to explore interesting conceptual features.

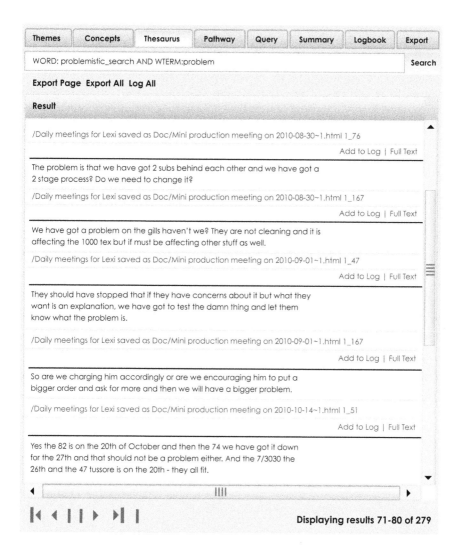

Themes	Concepts	Thesaurus	Pathway	Query	Summary	Logbook	Export

WORD: problemistic_search AND WTERM:problem | Search

Export Page Export All Log All

Result

/Daily meetings for Lexi saved as Doc/Mini production meeting on 2010-08-30~1.html 1_76

Add to Log | Full Text

The problem is that we have got 2 subs behind each other and we have got a
2 stage process? Do we need to change it?

/Daily meetings for Lexi saved as Doc/Mini production meeting on 2010-08-30~1.html 1_167

Add to Log | Full Text

We have got a problem on the gills haven't we? They are not cleaning and it is
affecting the 1000 tex but if must be affecting other stuff as well.

/Daily meetings for Lexi saved as Doc/Mini production meeting on 2010-09-01~1.html 1_47

Add to Log | Full Text

They should have stopped that if they have concerns about it but what they
want is an explanation, we have got to test the damn thing and let them
know what the problem is.

/Daily meetings for Lexi saved as Doc/Mini production meeting on 2010-09-01~1.html 1_167

Add to Log | Full Text

So are we charging him accordingly or are we encouraging him to put a
bigger order and ask for more and then we will have a bigger problem.

/Daily meetings for Lexi saved as Doc/Mini production meeting on 2010-10-14~1.html 1_51

Add to Log | Full Text

Yes the 82 is on the 20th of October and then the 74 we have got it down
for the 27th and that should not be a problem either. And the 7/3030 the
26th and the 47 tussore is on the 20th - they all fit.

Displaying results 71-80 of 279

Figure 3.10 Query tab

We mentioned previously that the researcher can manually provide concepts and
seed words that are of interest to her study. As this is the path that we chose for
the study, we explain it further in the following section.

Manual seeding of concepts

In many cases an automatically generated concept map, may contain concepts
that are irrelevant to the researcher's interests or may be lacking concepts that

they wish to locate in the text. That brings me to another powerful feature of Leximancer called *Profiling*. During the learning phase of the software, profiling discovers concepts associated with user-defined ones. This is useful for exploring issues in more detail, or adding a layer of more specific concepts, which expand upon a top layer of concepts. Profiling also allows the user to ignore large sections of text that are not relevant to their interests. In this study, all research questions aim to find links among various concepts. In the following sub-sections, we use research question RQ1a to demonstrate the steps followed in profiling our concepts. All remaining questions use the same process.

Step 1: disaggregate the research question

RQ1a: How do decision-making processes affect product creation processes?

We disaggregated the question to its basic constructs and concepts. The question has two constructs: (a) decision-making and (b) product creation. The decision-making construct includes the concepts of quasi resolution of conflict (RoC), organizational learning (OL), problemistic search (PS) and uncertainty avoidance (UA). The product creation construct contains the concepts of real-time market research (RTMR), and multiple collaborations (MC).

Step 2: identify synonyms

This step is performed for every concept. Each concept has the following structure:

- *Concept name* – the name of the concept
- *Concept definition* – concept definition as given by theory from which it is derived

We use the concept problemistic search and the literature derived definition as an example to demonstrate how this step works:

> Problemistic search is stimulated by a problem and is solution oriented. It is not about the generation of understanding nor is it driven by curiosity. It may be driven by conflict or by uncertainty avoidance.

There are some key words that strongly characterize this concept: **problem** and **solution**. To search all text just for these two key words alone would be over simplistic as they have many synonyms that could potentially be overlooked. Without providing those extra synonyms we have missed vital evidence relating to this concept. The next step was to identify all synonyms from *The Concise Oxford Thesaurus* (Kirkpatrick, 1997) so maximizing the chance of finding relevant text in the data. Table 3.1 identifies synonyms found for the words problem and solution.

Table 3.1 Concept problematic search and synonyms

Keyword	Synonyms
Problem	Problem, difficulty, complication, trouble, mess, predicament, plight, dilemma, dispute, puzzle, conundrum *We also chose to use the synonyms for the word 'problematic':* Tricky, uncertain, unsettled, questionable, debatable, arguable
Solution	Solution, answer, result, key, resolution, solving, resolving, explanation, clarification, elucidation, unravelling, unfolding

Step 3: profiling concepts

Using the *profiling* functionality of Leximancer, the concept, its key words and all synonyms are seeded in. Figure 3.11 demonstrates the Concept Seed Editor interface that allows the concept and all its synonyms to be fed into Leximancer.

Figure 3.11 Seed words for concept *problemistic* search

During the learning stage the software reads and rereads the corpus numerous times and identifies references where seed words are present. The software also discovers new words relating to the concept. At the end of this stage Leximancer produces a thesaurus which contains user seeded words as well as new words associated with the concepts and discovered through learning. Figure 3.12 provides a snapshot of the thesaurus generated for concept *problemistic search* with all words found and associated scoring.

The score shows the relevancy weightings associated with each indicative word. The higher the score the most relevant that word is to the concept and the most frequent that word appears in the text. The list of words is ordered in Score sequence (ascending or descending) but the user can change it to word order (ascending, descending). Seeded words that are not present in the text are not displayed.

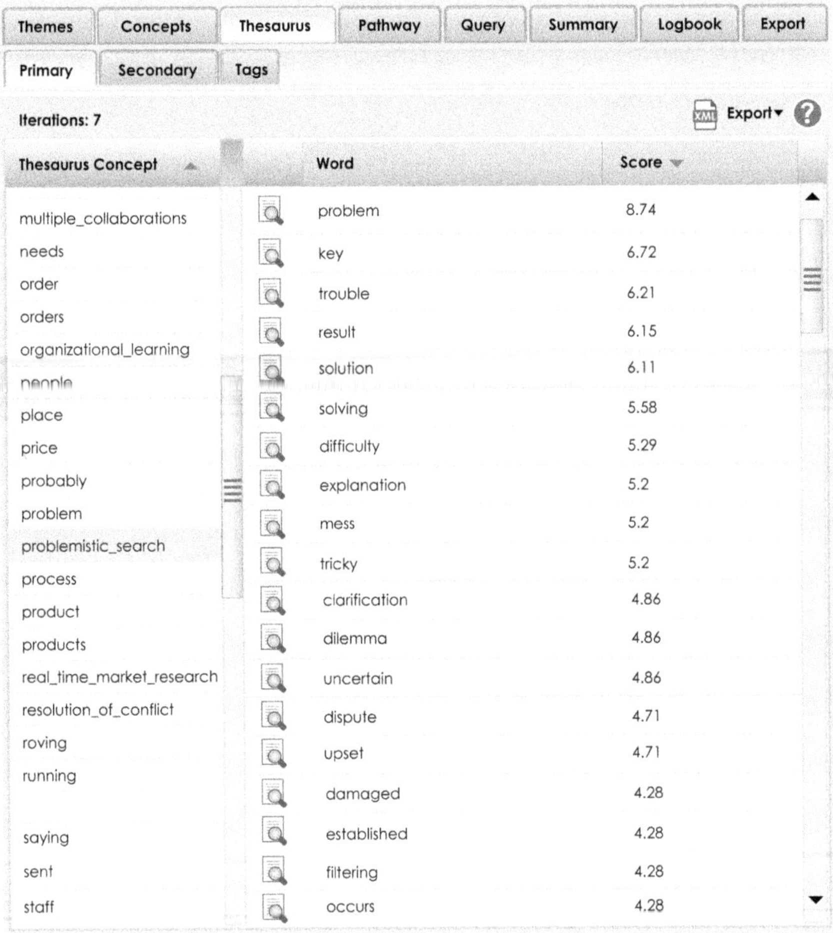

Themes	Concepts	Thesaurus	Pathway	Query	Summary	Logbook	Export

Primary	Secondary	Tags

Iterations: 7   XML Export▾ ❓

Thesaurus Concept ▲		Word	Score ▾
multiple_collaborations	🔍	problem	8.74
needs	🔍	key	6.72
order	🔍	trouble	6.21
orders	🔍	result	6.15
organizational_learning	🔍	solution	6.11
people	🔍	solving	5.58
place	🔍	difficulty	5.29
price	🔍	explanation	5.2
probably	🔍	mess	5.2
problem	🔍	tricky	5.2
problemistic_search	🔍	clarification	4.86
process	🔍	dilemma	4.86
product	🔍	uncertain	4.86
products	🔍	dispute	4.71
real_time_market_research	🔍	upset	4.71
resolution_of_conflict	🔍	damaged	4.28
roving	🔍	established	4.28
running	🔍	filtering	4.28
saying			
sent	🔍	occurs	4.28
staff			

Figure 3.12 Thesaurus generation for concept *problemistic* search

Step 4: omit missing synonyms

During this step, we revisited the list of synonyms for each concept. we cleaned the list of synonyms by deleting those that the software did not find. we could only work with the synonyms that we seeded. we could not change the ones that Leximancer discovered. For the *problemistic search* concept the following synonyms were either missing in the text or the accumulated evidence found was not enough to justify them being part of the concept: *answer, arguable, complication, conundrum, debatable, elucidation, plight, predicament, puzzle, solving, unfolding, unsettled*.

Step 5: delete noisy synonyms

During this step, we revisited the concept, and for every user seeded word we read all related text references. This is because sometimes synonyms can be used in different contexts and the results generated are too generic – this is what we refer to as 'noisy' synonyms. As Yin indicates this step helps clarify in what ways do codes or concepts accurately reflect the meaning of the retrieved words and phrases and why (Yin, 2009, p. 128).

Consequently, we looked at the text references from low score synonyms, which indicate that the number of text references is small. Following the same logic, we worked our way up to the high score synonyms. Having the concept definition in mind, if the text did not accurately reflect the meaning of the concept we deleted the 'offending', 'noisy' synonyms. For the *problemistic search* there were no 'noisy' synonyms. Therefore we demonstrate this step using as an example the concept *real-time market research (RTMR)*. From the definition of the concept the word *knowledge* was highlighted as being keyword and subsequently all synonyms were identified. One of these synonyms was the word *expertise*. Leximancer identified a single text reference for that synonym with no added value to the concept as the following example shows:

> "As I said before I am happy to be guided because it is not an area where we have the right level of expertise".

Another example for the RTMR was the synonym *place*. The text references associated with the *place* synonym add no value to the concept definition

> "Well it then will have to find its place, isn't it?" and
> "And that was how it was done in the first place", and
> "If it is the right place then we should make it happen".

Under these circumstances, there is no added value to the concept, moreover 'noisy' synonyms distort the findings, and we therefore deleted them. However, it is not always clear when a synonym should be kept or deleted. For instance, a synonym for *concept real-time market research* is the word *business*. When Leximancer searches for text containing the word *business* it picks up text such as

> "Anything else we need to cover? Any general business?"

It is apparent that the sentence does not add value to the definition of the concept. However, another sentence for the same word *business* does add value as WYM formulates the opinion through market research that Thailand is a safe place to do business with.

> "Talking about the upheaval in Thailand and whether it is a safe place to go for doing business".

We could not avoid these inconsistencies hence the procedure we followed was to count the text references of the value adding text for the word *business*. If that count was around 50 per cent or more of the total text references for the word *business*, then we considered the word as adding value to the concept and kept it. What we ended up with was a set of concepts each containing synonyms that closely related to the meaning of that concept.

Step 6: compound concepts

Using the same research question as previously (*RQ1a: How do decision-making processes affect product creation processes?*) we now explain in more detail how this step works.

Our goal was to link concepts and identify common text references. These references would equip me with the evidence we need to identify the existence or the lack of the previously concepts within our case study organization. All previous steps brought me closer to that. During the present step, we linked every concept from decision-making to all other concepts in product creation; effectively we ended up with twelve pairs of concepts for further analysis. This can be done using another powerful feature of Leximancer the *Compound* concepts feature. Figure 3.13 demonstrates the two concepts *organizational learning* and *real-time market research* ready to be compounded while Figure 3.14 shows the two concepts compounded. Compounded concepts appear with the conjunctive word 'and' between them (as seen in Figure 3.7).

The linking of selected concepts via Boolean operators obtains deeper and more meaningful analysis. The same process was followed for all remaining pairs in the research question.

Step 7: defining empirically derived concepts

Based upon these linkages between the theoretical concepts of decision-making, strategic product creation and sustainability outcomes, we systematically worked through the relevant text excerpts. From these excerpts, we defined empirically derived concepts where evidence of the co-occurrence of theoretical concepts existed within our data set.

Using the same research question as previously (*RQ1a: How do decision-making processes affect product creation processes?*) we now explain in more detail how this step works.

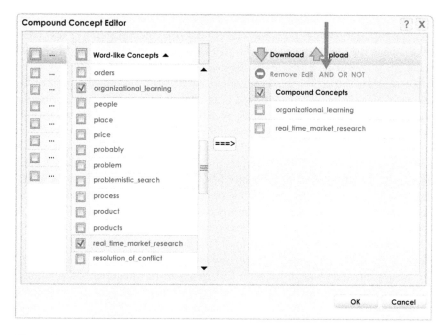

Figure 3.13 Compound concepts

Figure 3.14 Compound concepts

Real-time market research (RTMR) is a theoretical concept within the product creation processes. On its own, the concept has been identified in 841 text references. That is Leximancer found the synonyms for that concept and weighted them according to how frequently they occur in sentences. If enough evidence was accumulated then it tagged the sentences and presented them as part of the 841 references. When RTMR is linked to the decision-making concepts of organizational learning (OL), problemistic search (PS), uncertainty avoidance (UA) and resolution of conflict (RoC) it had 235, fifty-nine, twenty and seventeen co-occurring text excerpts respectively. That is the theoretical concepts of RTMR and OL co-occurred in 235 text references, RTMR and PS in fifty-nine, RTMR and UA in twenty-one and RTMR and RoC in seventeen text references. Looking closer at these common references, several areas that we refer to as empirical concepts emerged. For example, there were text excerpts concerned with how the firm incremented its knowledge through a feedback mechanism and hence we chose to organize these findings under the empirical concept of *learning from feedback*. In other occurrences, the uncertainty in developing products or acquiring new technology was at the fore, and we chose to categorize these findings under the empirical concept of *uncertainty in development*. Hence, for RTMR, we identified empirically derived concepts that emerged out of the intersection of this product creation concept and all decision-making concepts.

This analytical step was repeated for all co-occurring concepts.

Chapter summary

This chapter provided an understanding of the research process we engaged in. As a research strategy, we used a single-case study and employed qualitative research analysis to analyze our findings. We explained how we used the Leximancer text analytics qualitative software tool to produce robust results and enhanced the rigour of this study. We described in detail how Leximancer operates and provided seven comprehensive steps to follow for the analysis of the findings. In the next chapter, we put into action the seven steps and analyze the findings with the aim to answer the research questions.

Note

1 The concept names are the black wording appearing on the map.

References

Amaratunga, D., Baldry, D., and Sarshar, M. (2001). Process improvement through performance measurement: The balanced scorecard methodology. *International Journal of Productivity and Performance Management*, 50(5), 179–189. doi: 10.1108/EUM0000000005677.

Argote, L., and Greve, H. R. (2007). A behavioral theory of the firm – 40 years and counting: Introduction and impact. *Organization Science*, 18(3), 337–349. doi: 10.1287/orsc.1070.0280.

Eisenhardt, K. M. (1989). Building theories from case study research. *Academy of Management Review, 14*(4), 532–550.

Eisenhardt, K. M., and Graebner, M. E. (2007). Theory building from cases: Opportunities and challenges. *Academy of Management Journal, 50*(1), 25–32.

Flick, U. (2007). *Designing qualitative research.* London: Sage.

Golden-Biddle, K., and Locke, K. (2007). *Composing qualitative research* (2nd ed.). Thousand Oaks, CA: Sage.

King, G., Keohane, R. O., and Verba, S. (1994). *Designing social inquiry: Scientific inference in qualitative research.* Princeton, NJ: Princeton University Press.

Kirkpatrick, B. (1997). *The concise oxford thesaurus* (New ed.). Oxford University Press.

Langley, A., Van de Ven, A. H., Smallman, C., and Tsoukas, H. (2013). Process studies of change in organization and management. *Academy of Management, 56*(2), 1–13.

Marshall, C., and Rossman, G. B. (2006). *Designing qualitative research.* London: Sage.

Miles, M. B., and Huberman, A. M. (1994). *Qualitative data analysis.* Thousand Oaks, CA: Sage.

Rynes, S., and Gephart, R. P. (2004). From the Editors: Qualitative research and the "Academy of Management Journal". *Academy of Management Journal, 47*(4), 454–462.

Siggelkow, N. (2007). Persuasion with case studies. *Academy of Management Journal, 50*(1), 20–24.

Tsoukas, H., and Chia, R. (2002). On organizational becoming: Rethinking organizational change. *Organization Science, 13*(5), 567–582.

Yin, R. K. (2009). *Case study research design and methods.* Sage.

Yin, R. K. (2011). *Qualitative research from start to finish.* The Guilford Press.

4 Observations on decision-making, new product development and sustainability in a small business

This chapter presents the findings based on the analysis of the data collected at WYM. We revisit our research questions and for each one present empirically derived concepts and justify them with a range of examples extracted from our data set.

RQ1a decision-making and product creation

Decision-making construct encapsulates the theoretical concepts of organizational learning (OL), problemistic search (PS), uncertainty avoidance (UA) and resolution of conflict (RoC). When these concepts are linked to the product creation concepts of real-time market research (RTMR) and multiple collaborations (MC) there is indicative evidence that the case study organization constantly enriches its knowledge and learns from internal or external to the company feedback mechanisms. Learning also occurs when the firm partners and develops collaborative agreements with other firms. The findings also indicate that there is a degree of uncertainty caused either through developing new products or through technology enhancements or even through unstable market conditions. WYM is a customer-orientated firm, and the management team is regularly confronted with challenging customer behaviours.

Figure 4.1 demonstrates the concept map generated for RQ1a with all theoretical concepts as well as compounded concepts. Figure 4.2 displays the themes alone. In Figure 4.2 the 'hottest' theme is *real-time market research* as seen in dark grey in the figure (red in the colour diagrams on our website). As we move down the heat-map scale one would expect less relevant themes indicated by lighter greys (the 'colder' colours in the colour diagrams on our website). Concepts closely related to the theme *real-time market research* are *real-time market research* (RTMR) and *organizational learning* (OL) (see Figure 4.1).

RTMR is the highest-ranked concept among the product creation concepts identified in 841 text references. Moreover, the concept co-occurrence between RTMR and OL is the highest among all concept pairs with 235 common text references supporting the notion that companies learn using feedback mechanisms. These two concepts appear together often in the same pieces of text and attract one another strongly. Hence, they tend to settle near one another in the

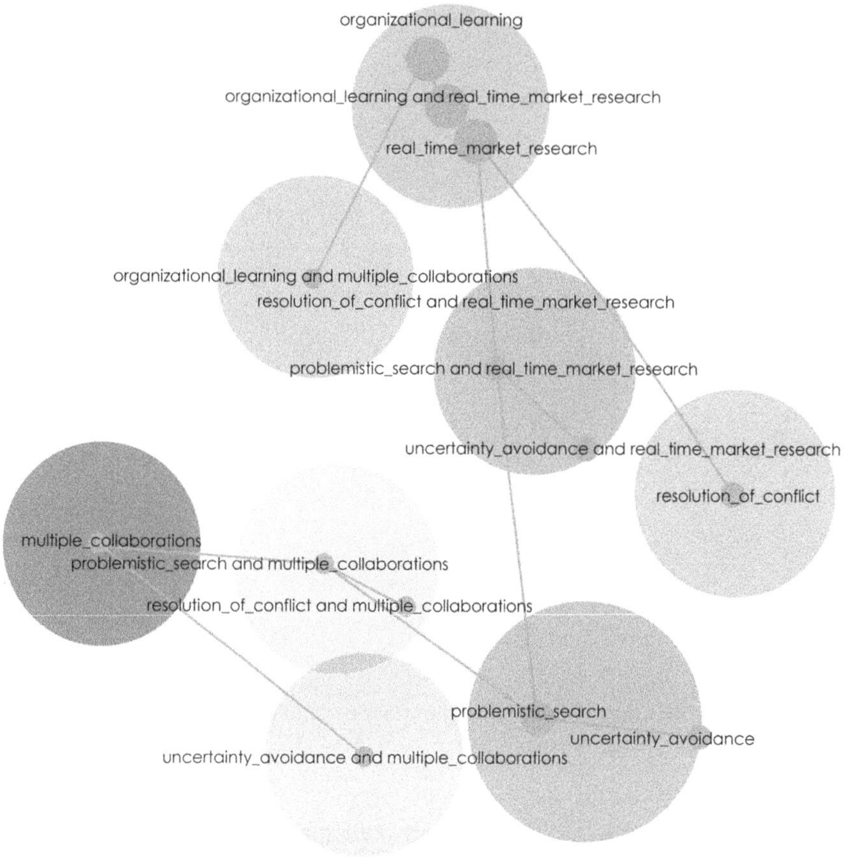

Figure 4.1 Concept map: how decision-making processes affect product creation processes

map space. A similar logic applies to the compound concept that also appears in the same map space. In this case, the compound concept *organizational learning and real-time market research* appear in the same map space as the concepts it is compounded from.

Figure 4.3 displays all concepts and compounded concepts for RQ1a in descending count order. RTMR dominates the top position among product creation and decision-making concepts with 841 text references, an indication that WYM applies RTMR as part of gathering information or harnessing customer preferences.

We present our results in a tabular format that allows us to see the big picture or identify a 'story' or a 'pattern'. Through linking concepts together, we have eight pairs for further analysis. In Table 4.1, the rows represent the product

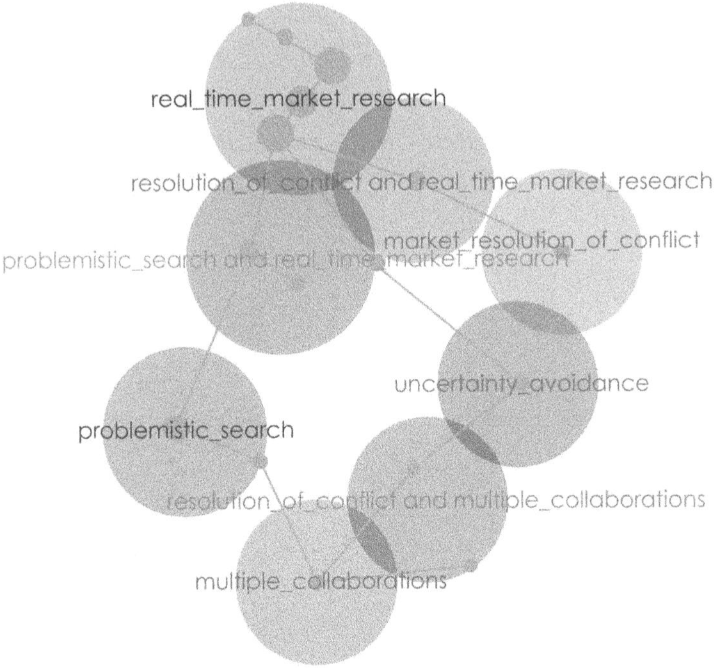

Figure 4.2 Themes map: decision-making processes and product creation processes

Word-Like	Count	Relevance	
real_time_market_research	841	100%	
organizational_learning	649	77%	
problemistic_search	480	57%	
organizational_learning and real_time_market_research multiple collaborations	235	28%	
uncertainty_avoidance	166	20%	
resolution_of_conflict	162	19%	
problemistic_search and real_time_market_research	99	12%	
uncertainity_avoidance and real_time_market_research	59	07%	
resolution_of_conflict and real_time_market_research	21	02%	
problemistic_search and multple_collaborations	17	02%	
organizational_learning and multiple_collaborations	13	02%	
resolution_of_conflict and multiple_collaborations	11	01%	
uncertainty_avoidance and multiple_collaborations	3	00%	
	2	00%	

Figure 4.3 Concepts for decision-making processes and product creation processes

Table 4.1 Decision-making and product creation common text references

	Quasi resolution of conflict (RoC)	Uncertainty avoidance (UA)	Problemistic search (PS)	Organizational learning (OL)
Real-time market research (RTMR)	17	21	59	235
Multiple short-term collaborations (MC)	3	2	13	11

Table 4.2 Decision-making concepts and text references

Quasi resolution of conflict (RoC)	Uncertainty avoidance (UA)	Problemistic search (PS)	Organizational learning (OL)
99	162	480	649

Table 4.3 Product creation concepts and text references

Real-time market research (RTMR)	Multiple short-term collaborations (MC)
841	166

creation concepts and the columns the decision-making concepts. Each cell contains the count of the common text references displayed previously in Figure 4.3. We also include the number of text references found for each decision-making and each product creation concept in Tables 4.2 and 4.3 respectively.

We now present the findings for the decision-making concepts. These only needs to be done once as the findings are identical for the first three research questions. It is important to analyze the text references for each individual concept as that provides evidence of its presence or absence as it might be at times in the case study organization.

Decision-making findings

In Table 4.2, we presented the decision-making concepts and their individual text references. Evidently organizational learning (OL) appears to be the most invoked and talked about concept from this construct with 649 text references. The thesaurus words that Leximancer generated for that concept contain words such as *information* with 128 hits, *thought* and *thinking* with 123 and ninety-eight hits respectively. These thesaurus words are ordered in word relevance with the most relevant words being closer to the top of the list. Less relevant are words such as *target* with thirty-nine hits, *attention* (twenty-six), *understanding* (twenty-five), *knowledge* (twenty-four) and *notice* (notice). However, what these words show is an appetite to increase the firm's knowledge, to acquiring more information, to understand how technology, processes work and to attend to goals in more effective ways.

Statements such as the following strengthen these findings (we use **bold** case for the indicative synonym):

> "The good thing is that we have sufficient **information** to start going to them", and
>
> "I think it is waiting for information but now I think we have enough **information** to write it down and do something about it, the same we do with the 1000 tex", and
>
> "I **thought** he said it went down (meaning the humidity) real fast", and
>
> "I think they say that the character of the product they got at the end is not the same as the originally supplied to them, I just **thought** let's wait and see the first of these colours run", and
>
> "They need a clear **understanding** of what the criteria need to be I think the only answer to that is just getting alongside them", and
>
> "It is also a good opportunity to increase some **knowledge** and skills and hope that anyone involved in that will enjoy it".

The second highest-ranked concept within the decision-making construct is the problemistic search (PS) with 480 text references. The top synonym here is *problem* with 279 text references. Other important synonyms are *key* (fifty-one), *trouble* (twenty-nine), *result* (twenty-seven), *solution* (twenty-six), *solving* (solving) and *explanation* (nine). All these synonyms indicate the raft of issues that WYM is faced with daily, and the efforts to alleviate them through launching to a problemistic search and finding solution to these issues. Next, we provide a set of representative examples of text references that indicate a problemistic search approach.

> "George says that this **problem** is not going to go away and we might need to hold some more merino on stock", and
>
> "The **problem** is that a length after carding (LAC) costs $400", and
>
> "That is fine, but it still leaves us with potential **problem** with that stuff right here (meaning the forward orders that they have to process). While they are saying that there might be a **problem** with our card and I am not disputing that, the **problem** of what we are supplied with is what I see it right from the beginning and it is too big a problem as it stands on its own", and
>
> "The **key** thing is that there are no new issues so we are heading in a good direction", and
>
> "For George the **key** thing is for the jobs to get up to date because they appear to be a little out of date on the board", and
>
> "The important thing is that you do not change too many things at once because then you don't know which thing made them improvements. Do one thing and then measure what the **result** is".

The third ranked concept within the decision-making construct is uncertainty avoidance (UA). Uncertainty can be generated through unsettling market conditions, or price fluctuations of raw wool sliver. The uncertainty is also caused internally either through processes that do not run to an expected high standard, or through a new product development the outcome of which is uncertain until the end of the development cycle. Hence it is important to report upon the approach that WYM's management team follows to mitigate these uncertain and risky factors. In this case, the most relevant synonyms are: risk (fifty-four), uncertainty (twenty-five), chance (twenty-three), avoid (sixteen), doubt (twelve), avoidance (eleven), pending (seven), unknown (seven). All these words indicate the presence of risk at WYM and show how they progress decision-making under uncertain conditions. What follows is a set of sample text where uncertain conditions are evidenced.

> "I am just looking at the bigger picture, we have got to be the same with our suppliers in regards to the fibre as well and if it is not long enough we say that it is too big of a risk", and
>
> "The other issue is that customer B have got some more ordered to be manufactured in the next month or so but because of the delay in payment there is a **risk** that the following orders will be pushed into the future", and
>
> "I am still confused with them because they want to change the count on the rovings by 50 and they still want to book ahead, don't they need to be doing that progressively? The reality is that there is a lot of **uncertainty** that creates issues", and
>
> "He is proposing that in order to **avoid** these long respond times from supplier QY they need to hold some undyed stock".

Finally, in the fourth place lies the concept of quasi resolution of conflict (RoC) evidenced in ninety-nine text excerpts. Conflict issues can occur within members of the same organization or externally with members of their supply chain. Looking at the relevant list of synonyms decision scores the highest with fifty-two text references. The word 'decision' is a synonym to the keyword 'resolution' emphasizing the approached that WYM seeks to resolve issues. Other synonyms are determine (nine), conflict (one), intention (two), struggle (two) and resolution (one). Some sample text follows.

> "So they still haven't made a **decision**, they changed the spec yesterday", and
>
> "We made a decision in here to change the date of that back and that was around customer C product developments and that stuff so there was a conscious decision to do that, and part of the **decision** was because it did not run that well and that is part of the reason we decided to push it back", and
>
> "Or you end up splitting your business because otherwise you will have conflict of short and long lead times and who is going to win is a short rover (like a 12 end one) something that you need for those sort of things?"

In summary, the findings around the decision-making concepts indicate that there is a great deal of organizational learning occurring in the case study organization. WYM also follows a problemistic search approach to resolve various firm issues. There is also evidence of how WYM management realizes and deals with uncertain conditions and to some extent there is evidence of resolving various challenging situations at WYM.

Decision-making and real-time market research

Real-time market research (RTMR) is the highest-ranked theoretical concept in product creation activities with the most text references (841). In that concept, the highest-ranked synonyms are the words *customer* (192), *business* (131), *market* (113), *information* (128), and *feedback* (seventy-nine). When linked to decision-making theoretical concepts RTMR and OL score 235 hits, RTMR and PS fifty-nine hits, RTMR and UA twenty-one hits and RTMR and RoC seventeen common references.

Through a systematic analysis of the common text excerpts, we defined empirically derived concepts where evidence of the co-occurrence of the theoretical concepts of decision-making and real-time market research existed within my data set. What follows is a presentation of these empirically derived concepts with representative examples for each one.

Learning from feedback

Feedback internal (within the company boundaries) or external (from customers, suppliers) is a powerful tool for assessing the performance of product developments. Particularly when a new product development make its way across the difficult factory operations (gilling, roving, production, drying, winding), feedback becomes hugely beneficial because it helps the product development team to identify 'hot spots' or problem areas, catch them early and fix them. The culture inspired from the general manager is that every new product development must have a 'drop dead' process flow:

> "Just going back to our product development process, we need **information** at every step and it has got to be a drop dead process".

A 'drop dead' process means that the products that reach a commercial launch stage are successful only if appropriate commercial acumen and technical skills are applied at every stage of the product development. 'Must have' criteria must be satisfied so that the product development can progress to the next stage. Enforcing best business practices oversees the production of a small carpet sample at first instance where the look and feel of a new product is tested. WYM strives for quality product at each stage of the operations; indeed, all their processes for driving new products to the market provide a testament to that quality:

> Quality product delivered to the **customer** each time, every time.

The customers' comments when they transform the yarn into a high-end carpet also merits attention; future product decisions heavily depend on customer feedback, in fact some of them even signal future product developments:

> "notes here that the **customer** was pretty happy and thanked WYM for doing it this way rather than sending goods that they were not finished properly", and
> "So in the first instance let's do one **questionnaire** and sent it out and gauge the response".

Lessons learned from previous product developments influence the way future products are being developed:

> "We get **feedback** today from customer C about the slab so hopefully put that to bed today".

Uncertainty in development

Product development forms a crucial part of WYM's operations. WYM endorses what is known as a '*stage-gate*' process (see Figure 3.2) where ideas or discoveries progress to commercial products in a quick and commercial manner; that is backing up products that are destined winners and nipping out products that cannot be supported by a business case. However, product developments include hidden risks; a brand-new product might require a change in a process, or certain machinery adjustments or even new technology. It is like a puzzle waiting to be done piece by piece:

> "working on the tower cans . . . measure the pressure . . . that will give us some indication how much extra drying capacity . . . better airflow . . . if successful we shall be increasing the number of cans that we put on the dryer".

Uncertainty in product development or in new technology is often where market research assists seeking answers and avoiding loopholes like in the following examples:

> "On that case it was a customer supplied product so we ring him and say that we are not able to process your product because of these reasons and the delivery is at **risk** because they have not supplied product suitable to us", and
> "It is too big **risk** for us to be carrying that out, unless it is a clear partnership, we say that from our partnership perspective it is not how we do best business practices, we need to start with small lots and work progressively to avoid any future issues".

The second example reflects the product development culture at WYM; the general manager enforces sound business practices and mitigates uncertainty through developing a small product sample, stress test it and progress to a commercial run. In that way, the performance is assessed internally and any potential issues identified and rectified early in the product development process:

> "I think we also need to say that we need to do 200 or 300kg at first and not 6 tonne to start with".

Another source of uncertainty is when customers delay signing order confirmations (SOC) which is the binding contract between customer and WYM; without a SOC there is a potential risk of the client changing the product specification (i.e. customer is less likely to change the product specification if they have already bound under the SOC contract):

> "So where is the signed order confirmation for that?"

Dealing with customer behaviours

WYM deals with a range of customers daily, some more professional than others:

> "this client has in the past been a bit difficult with payments hence careful consideration needs to be done here on how they approach them", and
> "We will be making the choice to see what we want to do in the case that he doesn't pay".

These customers are the exception than the norm. However, due to past product successes and increasing product demand for the niche market that WYM has carved, some customers impose demands beyond the capacity that WYM can satisfy. Translating these demands to finished products can be challenging:

> "there is no doubt about that and I think customer C is pleased for us to be doing plenty for them as well if you are talking to the operations side of the business", and
> "Needs to have a discussion with customer and need to see how they can **accommodate** this customer. An option is to have extra staff", and
> "Need a dedicated machine . . . to keep up orders with this prime customer".

Harness market opportunities

Product development plays a crucial role on maintaining future sales, business cash flow and market position. WYM constantly researches new market trends and opportunities, and makes sure that at least twice a year the general manager and the product development manager visit overseas clients. Specifically, European markets play an important role in new design styles:

> "The thing that we require is our ability to respond to new market **opportunities,** to create and design products that most traditional spinners cannot do", and

"Europe nevertheless is very important to us because Europe is the most demanding market in terms of style, design, quality and we must maintain that".

However, market instability, the financial meltdown during late 2008, currency fluctuations or raw wool price spikes is the cause of great concerns as the following show:

"They start the meeting by talking about currencies and the fact that most of the orders are in US dollars at the moment but they are also aware of the uncertainty of the euro in the European markets that they are dealing with", and

"I don't want to send them to PC prices and I see he has up the price by 20 cents? It is time to get a quote from someone else".

WYM aspires to produce products that are varied, technically demanding, well styled and difficult for competitors to copy. They seek brand differentiation and to establish a strong identity in the market place. This mentality is reflected in all parts of the business operations from attention to quality raw materials, to promoting good business practices among its customers, to establishing strong business partnerships:

"I think the key thing is that we are looking for established **business** and businesses that have been successful and businesses that run by people who are making it work, and I see that we have some good **opportunities** here".

Decision-making and multiple firm collaborations

The concept of multiple firm collaborations (MC) is not new. Firms network with other firms to improve their abilities to develop products, to acquire additional capabilities and to compete successfully in the market. MC is reflected in 166 text references with highest-ranked synonyms *capacity* (eighty-nine) and *capability* (twenty-seven). WYM depends heavily on collaborating with other firms allowing them to successfully perform their operations. From purchasing raw wool, to testing certain quality features of the wool sliver, to technology upgrades or improvements, WYM depends on other firms that offer complimentary capabilities and can strengthen their value chain. When linked to decision-making concepts MC and OL score eleven hits, MC and PS thirteen hits, MC and UA two hits and MC and RoC three hits.

Through a systematic analysis of the common text excerpts, we discovered empirically derived concepts where evidence of the theoretical concept co-occurrence existed within my data set. What follows next is a presentation of these empirically derived concepts with representative examples for each one.

Problem solving and learning through collaborations

WYM uses other firms' capabilities to perform various tests on product characteristics and production outcomes thereby increasing their product knowledge. In the following example the raw wool sliver length is tested using a process called length after carding (LAC). WYM uses a research institute to perform the LAC test as they do not have the necessary equipment to do it in-house:

> "Mentioning LAC and that they need to do it again and Paul agrees and says to take a sample out of the bin and sent it for checking".

In another example the exploratory learning surrounds an unusual production outcome:

> "In regards to the red stain in the CA batch, the research organization said that the red colouring washes out in solvent which indicates some kind of oil".

In both examples, collaborative learning occurs between WYM and a locally based government research organization.

Learning through troubleshooting are closely linked areas. At times, due to various reasons, the quality of the incoming raw sliver was below the standard required. In this situation, WYM performs their in-house tests to improve the quality of sliver and assess the success of each trial:

> "They are running this 1000 tex . . . they are having massive **problems** with that yarn . . . what is causing it?"

WYM also shares knowledge with customers who have expertise in the carding area. The following example is an advice given by the chief carding officer of a customer to WYM in regard to improving the carding process:

> "start measuring their CV at each point . . . pull yarn through my fingers . . . check the strength . . . and the thickness of it . . . you want to do that at each stage . . . it is all about continuous improvements, what will you do better tomorrow".

The learning also surrounds a potential purchasing decision:

> "They discuss potential acquisition of machinery that would be extremely useful to them. The machinery in mind is gills", and
>
> "the second gill line is making certain that there is plenty of gilling capacity and we can do 10 plus tonne easy as long as there are no other constraints", and
>
> "George says that they are meeting EC today to discuss new designs and pricings".

(EC is a local engineering company that designed and manufactured the new production machines and upgraded an existing one.)

As these examples indicate learning occurs through technology acquisitions and improvements. Another source of learning is generated through the potential creation of business partnerships:

> "What we decided the other day . . . we want to work a much closer relationship with the sheep breeder group".

In the last example, a desire to develop a supply partnership with a New Zealand sheep breeders group is indicated.

Mitigate supply chain uncertainty

When we examined the common text excerpts of these co-occurring concepts (decision-making concepts and MC) we observed a degree of uncertainty generated from seasonal price fluctuations in raw wool sliver that forces WYM to seek contracts with other suppliers. In the following example the supplier prices are unreasonably high, indicated by the general manager's comments:

> "I see he has up the price by another 20cents? It is time that we get a quote from someone else?"

In other instance the general manager aims to secure a supply contract when he says to a supplier:

> "You have to take a longer look and give us a whole season price or a 6-month price".

At times of heightened product demand, the in-house carding facility could not keep up with the demand hence other carding options are explored:

> "Who else can do some carding? Paul says QY, Mark says Lewis have carding capacity but Paul says the problem is that you cannot get more than 2 tonnes a day and we need more than that if we are running these colours", and
> "If Bill can't speed up we need to start ordering that sliver from the carding company now".

The general manager is adamant not to compromise quality over speed:

> "He is adamant that he wants someone with a proven track record of quality production".

Previous examples illustrate how certain risks are shared and potentially reduced through firm partnerships when product development takes place. Moreover, uncertainty caused by market instabilities (i.e. price fluctuations of raw materials) can be minimized through efforts of WYM management team to network with other firms that can provide complimentary capabilities.

Company document analysis

As we mentioned previously, the research questions were analyzed twice. The first time the analysis concentrated on all the meetings and interviewed data collected. The second time the analysis focused upon the company documents. The following tables (Tables 4.4, 4.5 and 4.6) identify the frequency of common text references in both meeting and interview data and in company documents.

It is of interest to note that like the meetings analysis the document analysis shows that the concept of RTMR on its own is the highest scoring among

Table 4.4 Decision-making and product creation common text references

		Quasi resolution of conflict (RoC)	Uncertainty avoidance (UA)	Problemistic search (PS)	Organizational learning (OL)
Real-time market research (RTMR)	Meeting and interview data	17	21	59	235
	Company documents	9	5	11	90
Multiple short-term collaborations (MC)	Meeting and interview data	3	2	13	11
	Company documents	0	0	0	4

Table 4.5 Decision-making concepts and text references

	Quasi resolution of conflict (RoC)	Uncertainty avoidance (UA)	Problemistic search (PS)	Organizational learning (OL)
Meeting and interview data	99	162	480	649
Company documents	23	14	52	202

Table 4.6 Product creation concepts and text references

	Real-time market research (RTMR)	Multiple short-term collaborations (MC)
Meeting and interview data	841	166
Company documents	398	31

the product creation concepts with 398 hits. Moreover, the co-occurrence of OL and RTMR is evidenced in ninety common text references. However, the concept of MC is less evident within the documents with thirty-one references and almost non-existent when linked to the decision-making concepts as seen in Table 4.4. Some text excerpts where RTMR intersects with decision-making concepts include:

"WYM desire flexible multi-skill thinking by operators and the management team. Therefore, position descriptions provide the typical in-house base but to be a responsive and innovative company all staff need to be willing to assist or develop skills as required", and

"Both forms can motivate employees: we all like to know we're doing well and generally people are receptive to information that will help them do a better job. After you have given feedback once, it is easier to give it (good or bad) a second time round", and

"The Quality Management System at WYM is intended give a brief overall of how the Quality Management System works, i.e. a series or process steps with details and requirements of that process step supported by training programmes and appropriate product information and checks", and

"Committed to delivering the solutions to customers (internal & external) need Learning as much as they can about our customers and use this information to change the way we run our business", and

"Production typically provides the application of technical skills in the carrying out of PD (Product Development) trials and variations. Competent staff (especially Senior Operators or Technical Specialists) at the various production stages apply know-how and record trial information including photos as appropriate".

How decision-making processes affect product creation processes at WYM

Before we proceed further in answering this and following research questions we explain how we rated the relationships among the various theoretical concepts. When we examined the relationships among the theoretical concepts, we rated some as strong, some as moderate and some as weak or non-existent. In this research, we define a strong relationship between two concepts one that demonstrates 50 per cent or above of common text references compared to the overall common references that arise from joining the theoretical strands out of which the concepts were derived. We refer to Table 4.4 to explain how this process works.

The total count of common text references between the decision-making and product creation constructs (the rows in yellow) is 361. Out of this, 332 references refer to the real-time market research concept being evidenced in the decision-making concepts. That means that 91 per cent of the overall common links refer to the relationship between the decision-making and the real-time market research theoretical concepts. This constitutes a very strong link. A moderate relationship is one that exhibits evidence in the range of 20–49 per cent. Anything below 20 per cent is regarded as weak or non-existent relationship. We found a similar pattern emerging from the findings of the company document analysis.

Hence across all product creation processes at WYM the strongest relationship occurs between decision-making processes and the concept of real-time market research. Of the four decision-making processes, organizational learning is the one that by far most commonly ties to real-time market research, followed by problemistic search, uncertainty avoidance and the quasi resolution of conflict.

The role of decision-making in real-time market research is clearly evidenced in learning from feedback, uncertainty in development, dealing with customer behaviours and harnessing market opportunities.

There is a weak relationship linking the multiple short-term collaborations concept to the decision-making processes with 9 per cent evidence. That said the role of decision-making in multiple collaborations is partly evidenced in problem solving and learning through collaborative practices and in mitigating supply chain uncertainty.

RQ1b decision-making and product strategy

When the four decision-making concepts of organizational learning (OL), problemistic search (PS), uncertainty avoidance (UA) and resolution of conflict (RoC) are linked to the product strategy concepts of speed to market (S2M), rapid performance upgrade through improved components (RPU) and proliferation of product variety (PPV) there is indicative evidence that WYM strives to improve production processes or improve technology with a view of making the work place operate more efficiently.

This also provides evidence of WYM dealing with challenging customer behaviours (as we have previously observed), particularly when they seek to improve the speed in which the finished yarn reaches their clients. There is also some evidence of how WYM management team mitigates uncertainty through harnessing various market opportunities.

Figure 4.4 demonstrates the concept map generated for decision-making processes and product strategy processes, which includes all theoretical concepts as well as all compounded concepts. Following a similar pattern to the previous research question, we present the themes alone in Figure 4.5. The 'hottest' theme is organizational learning. The theme takes its name from the concept organizational learning which scores the highest among these concepts with 649 text references. Co-occurring concepts in the theme are organizational learning and rapid performance upgrade (see Figure 4.4). The reason for this concept co-occurrence is because they appear together often in the same pieces of text, hence attract one another strongly and tend to settle near one another in the map space.

Figure 4.4 Concept map: decision-making processes and product strategy processes

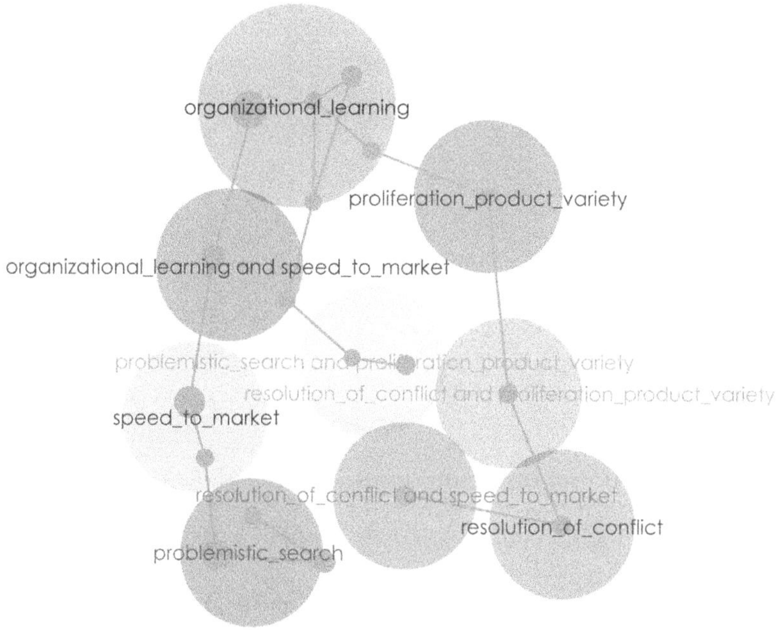

Figure 4.5 Themes map: decision-making processes and product strategy processes

Figure 4.6 displays all concepts and compounded concepts in descending count order. The compound concept *resolution of conflict* and *rapid performance upgrade* is missing as it has no common references. As seen in Figure 4.6, *speed to market (S2M)* is the most relevant concept in product strategy identified in 403 text references followed by rapid performance upgrade (RPU) with 161 references and proliferation of product variety (PPV) with 131 text references.

Table 4.7 presents the linked pairs between decision-making and product strategy concepts. As seen again here, S2M and RPU concepts score the highest when linked to the decision-making concepts with thirty-three and thirty-two common text references respectively. Table 4.8 presents the number of text references for the product strategy concepts.

Decision-making and speed to market

Speed to market (S2M) otherwise known as 'lead time' is identified within 403 text references and it is the highest scoring concept among the product strategy concepts. The highest found synonyms are the words *lead* (142), *speed* (seventy-nine), *quick* (forty-seven), *fast* (thirty-nine) and *times* (166). The word *times* was learned through the Leximancer learning stage. Numerous other words make up for the rest of the text references. When linked to the decision-making concepts

Word-Like	Count	Relevance
organizational_learning	649	100%
problemistic_search	480	74%
speed_to_market	403	62%
rapid_performance_upgrade	161	25%
uncertainty_avoidance	161	25%
proliferation_product_variety	131	20%
resolution_of_conflict	99	15%
organizational_learning and speed_to_market	33	05%
organizational_learning and rapid_performance_upgrade	32	05%
problemistic_search and speed_to_market	21	03%
organizational_learning and proliferation_product_variety	14	02%
uncertainty_avoidance and speed_to_market	13	02%
problemistic_search and rapid_performance_upgrade	8	01%
resolution_of_conflict and profileration_product_variety	6	01%
problemistic_search and profileration_product_variety	5	01%
resolution_of_conflict and speed_to_market	4	01%
uncertainty_avoidance and profileration_product_variety	3	00%
uncertainy_avoidance and rapid_pertormance_upgrade	1	00%

Figure 4.6 Concepts for decision-making processes and product strategy processes

Table 4.7 Decision-making and product strategy linked pairs

	Quasi resolution of conflict (RoC)	Uncertainty avoidance (UA)	Problemistic search (PS)	Organizational learning (OL)
Speed to market (S2M)	4	13	21	33
Rapid performance upgrading through improved components (RPU)	0	1	8	32
Proliferation of product variety (PPV)	6	3	5	14

Table 4.8 Product strategy concepts with count of text references

Speed to market (S2M)	Rapid performance upgrade (RPU)	Proliferation product variety (PPV)
403	161	131

S2M and OL appear in (thirty-three) common textual references, S2M and PS in (twenty-one), S2M and UA in (thirteen) and S2M and RoC in (four) common text.

We analyzed the common text excerpts, and defined a range of empirically derived concepts where evidence of the co-occurrence of theoretical concepts existed within my data set. Next, we present these empirically derived concepts with representative examples for each one.

Dealing with customer behaviours

S2M is a key performance indicator for the business measured each week during the production meetings. Customers often require product at very short timeframes and if the S2M is persistently low (i.e. product takes longer to reach customer) eventually customers cease to order products as the general manager comments in one of the meetings:

> "We are going to pull in a competitor very **soon**", and
> "draws the attention to the list of products that Customer C has placed upon WYM and that it has been agreed so they need to make sure that they can deliver them the **times** they agreed to", and
> "Here they are talking about Customer L and Carol stresses the fact that the customer is screaming at the moment about having his stuff over there".

S2M reflects production efficiencies; how fast can the product be manufactured and delivered. As production is often hindered by external factors (i.e. raw materials delay or poor quality, dying wool sliver depends on dying firm's flexibility) or internal factors (i.e. inefficient processing due to poor quality raw materials, machine capacity not enough for the increasing product demand), speed becomes even more critical for the business as the general manager argues here:

> "A day late will be a severe beating; a **week** later would be an execution".

The management team is aware that delivery times agreed with customers must be honoured; even the slightest delay causes serious concerns as the general manager queries:

> "Is there anything else that can be done in catching up during the forthcoming **week**?"

Good business practices help mitigate uncertainty; for example, job planning and prioritizing on the board and clear communication with supply chain partners on what/when is expected from either party as in the following examples:

> "They also talk about raw materials (sliver) and that it needs to be delivered in plenty of **time** ahead", and
> "Here George explains to Kathy why he needs the sliver earlier rather than later".

The team often brainstormed ideas on improving production efficiencies:

> "The general manager wants to get the factory back to be up to date and he asks the production manager advice on that".

Furthermore alternative (quicker) roots to sending product to customer were explored:

> "This has got to go by bullet (very **fast**)".

Sometimes WYM was willing to airfreight product:

> "I am happy to airfreight samples so we can turn feedback loop quicker".

Improve process

When the management team revisits processes with a view of making them more efficient, there are some positive outcomes generated. An example is when the manufacturing process required manually filling in paperwork to record the daily production in tonnes of yarn. The staff operating the production machines manually record the quantity (in kilograms) of specialty yarn produced daily. However, it came to the attention of the management team that this manual paperwork recording was not always consistent and information was at times missing leading to uncertainty and errors:

> "There is an incomplete information and it needs immediate attention otherwise I don't know what has been done, it needs a discipline there because if that is the main driver for the factory and we don't even know that it is ticking over, that concerns me".

So, the team revisited that process and decided to automate it. Instead of manually recording the tonnage, the central production machine through adjusting a machine setting automatically can do that.

Another area was to create a proactive thinking referring to the disposal of the waste generated. Moreover, for various items that are otherwise difficult to obtain (merino wool) they can hold some safety stock as the following examples indicate:

> "Primarily they need to solve their bottlenecks at any one time, also the rubbish bins should be emptying not when the lead does not close any more but part of the smart thinking would be to do it along the way", and
>
> "The general manager is proposing that in order to avoid these long respond times from Supplier QY they need to hold some undyed stock".

When new product developments take place, the thinking is to always develop a small sample, assess the performance, learn from it, even involve the customer if needed, and then if all criteria are satisfied, only then progress to commercial production. That way the turnaround feedback is quick and inevitably the whole process will run smoother:

> "We are sending them some frieze at the moment and they are saying that it is a bit lively so it is exactly what we are doing here and I am keen to push smaller batch size then we can identify quicker if we have difficulties and change the settings".

Improve technology

The increasing appetite of customers for WYM's specialty yarn prompted them to look into expanding manufacturing capacity. Learning also increased when evaluating options around speeding up production. Technology improvements and speed to market are closely linked as more machinery means that the production of yarn would increase hence meeting customer expectations and reducing the 'lead time' that product takes to reach customer. Some examples where machinery acquisitions and operational changes were discussed are listed here:

> "Basically this meeting took place at RYT between the two parties in order to discuss the ever so urgent now design and manufacturing of the new machine F40 which needs to be installed in the factory as soon as possible as orders are coming thick and fast", and

"We have got heaps of specialty yarn to do, so obviously we are looking at R32Z and we have identified the problem where it is getting a fault", and

"We can only do that one step at a time. The engineering firm is talking more around here (showing a date on the board) and at this stage that is our immediate obstacle and we have to work with customer D and hopefully get back to them by tomorrow once I have chance to get back with engineering firm between today or tomorrow so we can give them some answers".

The firm improved production efficiencies further when they installed the new tower cans which had increased capacity, thereby drying more yarn in less time:

"We had double doffs and even triple doffs into some . . . and only increasing the drying time by another 30 per cent".

Doff as referred to here as a load of product. Double doff means that two loads of product fit where only one used to fit before the tower cans were introduced.

Decision-making and rapid performance upgrade

The concept of rapid performance upgrade (RPU) was evidenced in 161 text references with highest-ranked synonym *progress* (eighty-nine). When linked to decision-making, RPU and OL score (twenty-eight), RPU and PS (eight), RPU and UA (one) common text references. Through a systematic analysis of the common text references we derived the following empirical concepts where RPU and decision-making coexist and present next.

Improve technology

Technology improvement through machinery upgrades or through purchasing additional equipment is necessary to do the job. While new machinery acquisition helped WYM to cope with a heightened product demand, technological improvements to existing machines were also important, as mentioned in the following discussion:

"Discussing potential acquisition of machinery . . . gills", and
"They are welding up the F28 . . . to avoid the problem with product quality", and
"Also the plumbing needs sorting . . . there was a lot of sludge at the bottom".

An innovative project that WYM undertook during the time of this research and provided a constant source of learning for the company was the 'tower cans' project.[1] Tower cans replaced the old storage cans over time and resulted in large energy savings as the drying time decreased by 50 per cent:

"The 6kg they were dying in about two to 2.5 hours so there is easy a 50 per cent improvement".

When the tower cans project was instantiated, the general manager urged the staff:

> "To experiment with those and work out what is required . . . if that works then I would like to see another 80 or 120 towers".

Another effort was made in reducing the quantity of water effluent disposed during the production process. Continuous trials ensured that the effluent reduced while still maintaining the same quality on the finished product. Innovative thinking also occurred during the development of some gadgets to fulfil various product requirements as mentioned here:

> "Need some engineering development to wrap the string around the yarn somehow".

Improving existing machine components when for example the yarn was sticking in the production machinery:

> "Rubber rollers stick and the yarn is sticking and wrapping around them".

Improve process

Process improvement can trigger technology improvements. For example, to improve the quality of the sliver, trials in the initial stages of wool processing – the carding process- were also explored as the product design manager indicates here:

> "One thing we haven't tried is to open up the settings on the card, so those things need to be explored".

WYM was also keen to get advice on the matter from one of their prime customers who had additional expertise in the carding area. Trials consist of increasing the number of roving passes[2] *or* incorporating combed wool into the raw wool as the following snippets suggest:

> "It had four passes and it has been up twisted", and
> "Are we going to use combed top?"

There was an issue surrounding the winding process so George instantiated a search for a solution:

> "The general manager is keen to put this problem with the winding somewhere in order to be sorted sooner rather than later".

Carrying on from previous example he initiated a search situation that resulted in new machinery:

> "He is asking if it can be solved by new machinery or by something else".

Another source of rapid performance upgrade was the customer feedback, in one occasion it was around product quality:

> "We had a little advisory from cavalier about the slabs and I was wondering if we could use combed top".

Harness market opportunities

Identify and harness market opportunities can reduce uncertainty about future customer demand or market preferences as the following examples indicate:

> "The thing that we require is our ability to respond to new market opportunities, to create and design products that most traditional spinners cannot do. People come to us because we can create new products", and
>
> "We need to go through outline some of the physical process of blend development and then we need to explore the market opportunities where this should be placed and also bearing in mind your long-term expectations".

Decision-making and proliferation of product variety

The concept of proliferation of product variety (PPV) is found in 134 text references with highest-ranked synonyms *sample* (eighty-three) and *variety* (seventeen). Sample yarn is linked to new product development. This is an essential step to identify potential issues early in the development stages of a new product. When linked to decision-making practices PPV and OL appear in (eight), PPV and PS in (six), PPV and UA in (three) and PPV and RoC in (six) common text references. From all common references the most informative ones are the ones linked with learning. Undoubtedly learning occurs through troubleshooting and solving operational issues when product development work is taking place as the following suggest:

> "I have told Colin to hold those other product developments till further notice pending from customer feedback", and
>
> "He points out another problem with customer D who has problems running the yarn that WYM sent them and he talks about doing an emergency product development of high twist and low degree of 3600 tex along the lines of the product development they just shipped to them. If they have that to them by Monday or Wednesday next week they will be able to discuss it with them – they are looking at about. 5kg of sample so he has to look doing that today", and
>
> "He then mentions the fact that in order to maintain good times for the customer F job – he has talked in the past about cutting the job into smaller manageable junks".

At the same token uncertainty is always visible when new products are being ordered:

> "At this stage again they are reworking the board to cater for uncertainty from customer C and to push other jobs in the slot there. So the winners out of this rearrangement is customer U, somebody else and Nick's rugs".

Company document analysis

The findings from the meeting/interview analyzed data are compared with the findings from the document analysis data. Tables 4.9, 4.10 and 4.11 provide common text references as well as individual concept text count.

It is of interest that S2M scores the highest among product strategy concepts followed closely by RPU. There is limited evidence of the presence of the PPV concept in the documents (seven hits) (refer to Table 4.11) and some evidence of RPU and S2M concepts when linked to the decision-making concepts. Some examples follow here:

> "Maintain a lead time of appropriate for the products design process and able to meet customer expectations", and

Table 4.9 Decision-making and product strategy common text references

		Quasi resolution of conflict (RoC)	Uncertainty avoidance (UA)	Problemistic search (PS)	Organizational learning (OL)
Speed to market (S2M)	Meeting and interview data	4	13	21	33
	Company documents	0	1	2	7
Rapid performance upgrading through improved components (RPU)	Meeting and interview data	0	1	8	32
	Company documents	1	0	2	9
Proliferation of product variety (PPV)	Meeting and interview data	6	3	5	14
	Company documents	0	0	0	5

Table 4.10 Decision-making concepts and text references

	Quasi resolution of conflict (RoC)	Uncertainty avoidance (UA)	Problemistic search (PS)	Organizational learning (OL)
Meeting and interview data	99	161	480	649
Company documents	23	14	52	202

Table 4.11 Product strategy concepts and text references

	Speed to market (S2M)	Rapid performance upgrading through improved components (RPU)	Proliferation of product variety (PPV)
Meeting and interview data	403	161	131
Company documents	46	34	7

"If the production is right up with the prerequisite process and no buffer sheets are currently on the board then there will be indicator cards (Red Cards) to match the expected production priority/order to mirror the Main Production Planning Board in the Production Office. No Buffer sheets may also mean that the prerequisite processes need extra attention to get up to speed to avoid stopping the constraint point", and

"The Production Buffer Management Board purpose is to visually display the production requirements of each day through the production process. By having production visually displayed on this board, each operator can track progress of production expectations and along with their Team Leader make recommendations to take action if we are falling behind or well ahead of production requirements".

How decision-making processes affect product strategy processes at WYM

The total count of common text references between decision-making and product strategy constructs is 140.

From the 140 common text references 50 per cent of these refer to the theoretical concept of speed to market being evidenced in the decision-making processes. Hence that signifies a strong link between the decision-making and speed to market theoretical concepts. The relationships between decision-making and rapid performance upgrading is moderate with 29 per cent evidence. The relationship between decision-making and proliferation of product variety is also moderate with 20 per cent evidence. Far fewer common references emerge in the findings from the document analysis however similar patterns also exist here.

Hence across all product strategy processes at WYM the strongest relationship occurs between decision-making processes and speed to market. Of the four decision-making concepts, organizational learning is the one most commonly linked to speed to market and to rapid performance upgrade.

The role of decision-making in speed to market is evidenced when dealing with customer behaviours or when improving production processes and technology.

The role of decision-making in rapid performance upgrade is evidenced in process and technology improvements.

Finally, the concept of proliferation of product variety is mainly evidenced around organizational learning.

RQ1c decision-making and central strategy

We link the four decision-making concepts of organizational learning (OL), problemistic search (PS), uncertainty avoidance (UA) and resolution of conflict (RoC) to the central strategy concepts of strategic flexibility (SF), fixed asset parsimony (FAP) and modular product architecture (MPA). The findings show similar evidence to RQ1b in that WYM strives to improve production processes or improve technology to increase production efficiencies. In addition, there is indicative evidence that WYM strives to maintain a competitive advantage over their competitors. However, there is a profound lack of evidence that modular product architecture exists at WYM.

Figure 4.7 demonstrates the concept map generated for RQ1c with all concepts and compounded concepts. Figure 4.8 displays the themes alone. In Figure 4.9 the 'hottest' theme is *organizational learning* as seen in red. Co-occurring concepts in this theme are concepts *organizational learning* and *fixed asset parsimony* with fifty-nine text references.

In Figure 4.9, we display all concepts and compounded concepts in descending count order. The *strategic flexibility* (SF) concept scores the highest among the central strategy concepts evidenced in 328 text references. *Fixed asset parsimony* (FAP) is evidenced in seventy-four references however there is a significant absence of the *modular product architecture* (MPA) concept within our data set and hence a profound lack of evidence linking decision-making to MPA. Therefore, the four pairs linking decision-making to MPA are all missing.

We present the results in a tabular form (Tables 4.12 and 4.13). SF is the highest-ranked concept among the central strategy concepts with 328 hits. There are no links between decision-making and modular product architecture concepts indicated by "0" in the cells.

The following sections present the findings on the various links.

Decision-making and strategic flexibility

The concept of strategic flexibility (SF) has the most text references within the central strategy activities (328). The highest found synonyms are the words *opportunity* (157), and *competitive* (twenty-eight). Numerous other words make

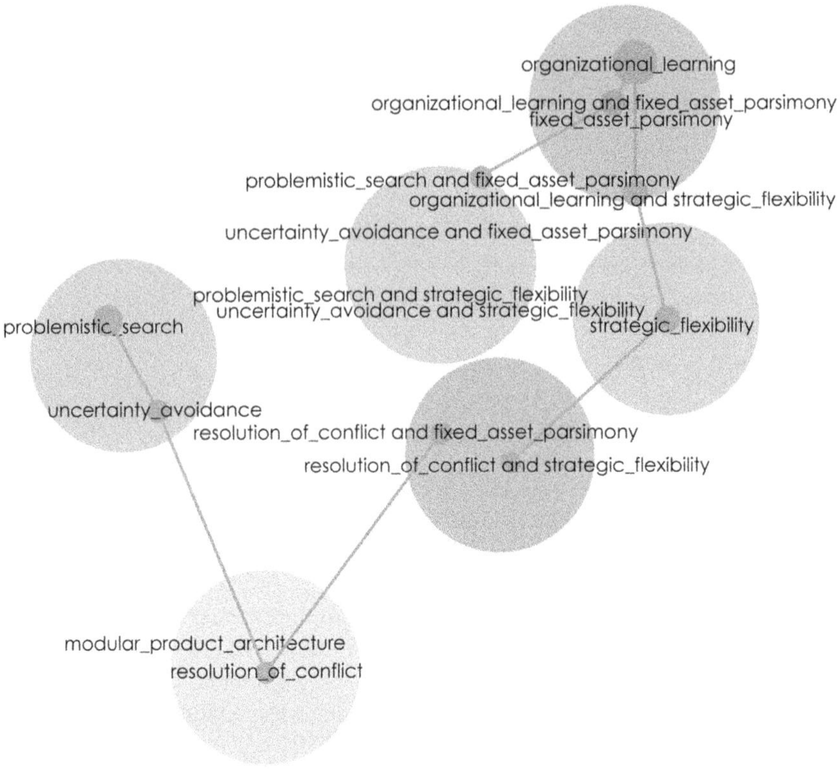

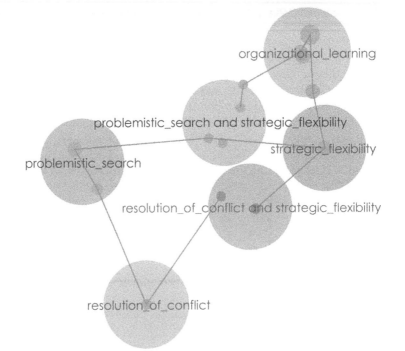

Figure 4.7 Concept map for decision-making and central strategy

Figure 4.8 Themes map for decision-making and central strategy

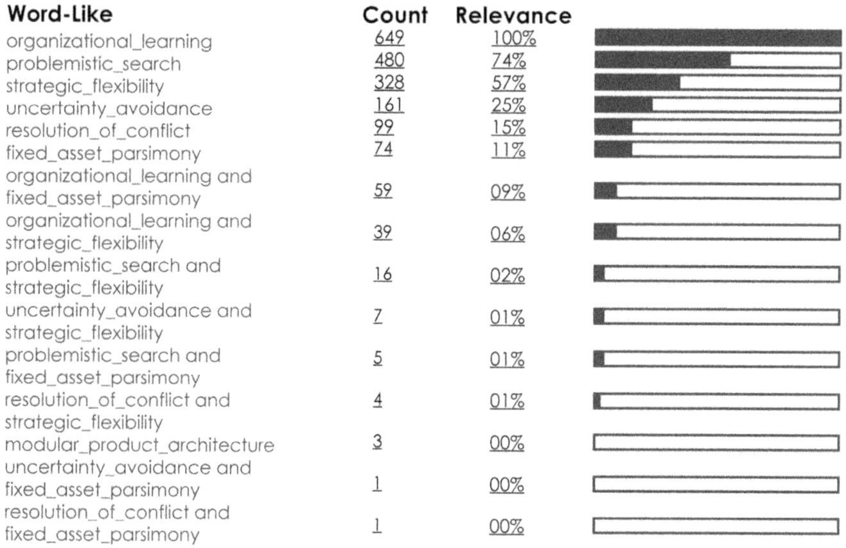

Word-Like	Count	Relevance	
organizational_learning	649	100%	
problemistic_search	480	74%	
strategic_flexibility	328	57%	
uncertainty_avoidance	161	25%	
resolution_of_conflict	99	15%	
fixed_asset_parsimony	74	11%	
organizational_learning and fixed_asset_parsimony	59	09%	
organizational_learning and strategic_flexibility	39	06%	
problemistic_search and strategic_flexibility	16	02%	
uncertainty_avoidance and strategic_flexibility	7	01%	
problemistic_search and fixed_asset_parsimony	5	01%	
resolution_of_conflict and strategic_flexibility	4	01%	
modular_product_architecture	3	00%	
uncertainty_avoidance and fixed_asset_parsimony	1	00%	
resolution_of_conflict and fixed_asset_parsimony	1	00%	

Figure 4.9 Concepts for decision-making and central strategy

Table 4.12 Decision-making process and central strategy common text references

	Quasi resolution of conflict (RoC)	Uncertainty avoidance (UA)	Problemistic search (PS)	Organizational learning (OL)
Strategic flexibility (SF)	4	7	16	39
Fixed asset parsimony leveraged intellectual assets (FAP)	1	1	5	59
Coordination through modular product architecture (MPA)	0	0	0	0

up for the rest of the text references. The principles of SF and OL appear in (thirty-nine), SF and PS in (sixteen), SF and UA in (seven) and SF and RoC in (four) common text references. Examining these common references systematically we derived a set of empirically defined concepts where SF and decision-making concepts coexist within the case study organization.

Table 4.13 Central strategy concepts with count of text references

Strategic flexibility (SF)	Fixed asset parsimony (FAP)	Modular product architecture (MPA)
328	74	3

Improve technology

From a technology standpoint, any machinery upgrades or improvements assisted the business to maintain competitive advantage and leadership in the specialty yarn industry

> "Talking again about the importance of getting the production machine upgraded".

When lead times were high, the management team acutely aware of the importance of the situation explored other options such as machinery upgrades or employ more staff

> "He says that they need to work out what they can do by a certain time . . . they don't see that as a balloon and they need to increase their whole level to a new platform. The general manager then says there are some **opportunities** with the new machine and some new staff coming".

Improve process

Various process improvements took place during the time we collected our data. In daily operations, good planning and job prioritizing maximizes machine efficiencies,

> "Making certain there is buffer for the machines and the ability to go at full speed".

Furthermore, when new product development took place, prudence dictated to start by developing a small sample product. Forward thinking allowed the firm to hold a safety stock of certain raw materials (i.e. merino wool) to avoid future shortages. In one of the board meetings a member argued that an immediate response to reducing lead times would be to increase the operating hours.

> "We have to adopt an urgency approach and see how do we cover the position in the short term till the end of September so our lead times begin to decrease and the only way I can see do that is to increase hours".

From then onwards the management team went on to increase the roving hours to twenty-four hours, five days a week, an approach that worked as it stabilized the lead times in the short-term.

Strategic flexibility demonstrated in the joint efforts to create a supply chain with a sheep breeders group so that they could promote a 'green story' for their supply chain, however this joint venture did not materialize at the end:

"We can start initializing business with HW group".

However firm knowledge increased when the partnership with a sheep breeders' group was discussed:

"The genetics is how we differ to anyone else in NZ. We are in control right from the start and can have that as part of any story . . . it must be the WYM breeding objective for wool and it is worth it, we can offer that".

Maintain a competitive advantage

The findings indicate that WYM evaluated market conditions regularly and examined ways to remain competitive under fluctuating market conditions or future market uncertainties. In fact the concept of strategic flexibility represents a fundamental approach to managing uncertainty (Sanchez, 1995, p. 138). For instance, the increase in the price of the raw wool sliver prompted the team to search for alternative supplier sources as the following examples suggest:

"I see he has up the price by another 20 cents . . . it is time to get a quote from someone else".
"I was just thinking last night that in terms of our competitive advantage the way the currency is now we are probably about 10 per cent less competitive than we were because against all of the currencies we are selling to we are at an all time high, euro, US".

Another example of remaining competitive is the way WYM handled challenging customer behaviours. Challenging customers most commonly appearing to delay payments, or withholding part of the payment or not signing a changed product specification order form (SOC)[3] also generated uncertainty, however WYM management did their best to enforce good business practices such as refusing to process their orders unless there is a SOC received:

"WYM needs confirmation from his bank that they have paid . . . he refuses to let the container leave without any money", and
"Customer C is also asking for a lot and we need to talk to them more about how it all fits in".

The ability of WYM to select customers that fit their profile is also demonstrated in the following text excerpt:

"The thing that we require is our ability to respond to new market opportunities, to create and design products that most traditional spinners cannot do. People come to us because we can create new products. And the strategic intend is to seek customers that fit at the top end of the broadloom market. That is the strategic banner we are heading towards. This is what will give us a competitive edge".

Decision-making and fixed asset parsimony

The concept of fixed asset parsimony (FAP) appears in seventy-four text references. There was considerable interest in protecting the intellectual property rights applying to new production technology at WYM. The highest found synonyms for that concept are words *knowledge* (twenty-four), *intellectual* (sixteen), *learning* (fifteen) and *IP* (fifteen). The concepts of *fixed asset parsimony* and *organizational learning* have common synonyms as they both refer to knowledge acquired and incremental learning practices. Hence the co-occurrence between FAP and OL concept of decision-making processes was evidenced in fifty-nine common references. Next, we present the empirically derived concept where decision-making and FAP coexist.

Improve process

The deteriorating quality of the incoming raw wool sliver prompted WYM to explore alternative supplier sources and increment the firms' knowledge:

> "Talking about the possibility of getting longer fibre for the whole of the product range . . . and looking into south island suppliers for that".

The poor quality or raw wool also ties with the concept of FAP were various tests were performed to determine the issues around the poor quality. The push for quality is reinforced through the OFI system where a record for each quality issue is opened and all the steps to rectify the issue are recorded. The 'competitive manufacturing' initiative that took place during the time of this study also reinforced the need for:

> "Good communication, team management and people understanding the processes, products, strategies and customers of the firms".

That way they can understand the big picture and make intelligent decisions in their areas

> "So if I was to measure a level of competency we should be asking questions from previous managed event tasks because that is making certain that we get our existing knowledge ingrained into our brains".

The machine 'guardian' concept (the idea that a member of staff will be expert of a certain process) also ties in with the concepts of FAP and OL as the following indicates:

> "It all fits into the machine guardian scope because you need to have this knowledge to be a machine guardian and he needs to be a senior operator

and have the operator level thinking. So we have got background out there but we need to give the time and opportunity for these operators to build up that knowledge and George wants to see that benchmarked so they know what to do".

For monitoring the production, WYM utilized a computer system as well as visual monitoring boards: release board, buffer management board and despatch control board. Each one served a specific function and kept track of jobs released, produced and dispatched. An issue was raised with the buffer management board as the following example identifies which also linked the fixed asset parsimony to problemistic search concepts:

> "Communication is also very important and the buffer board needs a drastic change as it is not currently working. Level of **knowledge** is also important and the attitudes of people towards solving **issues** rather than running to the team leaders and asking them what to do".

A potential conflict also emerged in connection to the intellectual property (IP) rights for the production technology. The conflict reflected a hazy area of who owns the IP rights – is it WYM or the engineers who developed the machinery?

> "As part of this deal we need to enter into a contractual agreement with EF about ownership with the intention of retention of the intellectual property (**IP**) and that comes part of the asset transfer. Because all of a sudden we now have the state of the art world leading specialty yarn production technology and that is now capable of being replicated very easily".

Decision-making and modular product architecture

There is no evidence to show that modular product architecture (MPA) exists at WYM.

This is indicated by the minimal number of hits that MPA scored (three) as well as the absence of common text references when linking decision-making to the MPA concept as seen in Table 4.12. Hence, we conclude that modularity was non-existent in the case study organization.

Company document analysis

The findings from the data collected from meetings were compared with the findings from the document analysis. Tables 4.14, 4.15 and 4.16 provide common text references as well as individual concept text count. The rows in yellow present the common text references from the analysis of the meeting and interview data as seen in previous sections. The rows in pink present the common text references for the analysis of the company documents.

The strategic flexibility concept focuses on creating managerial and organizational competences capable to respond quickly to a range of future changes. As

Table 4.14 Decision-making and product strategy common text references

		Quasi resolution of conflict (RoC)	Uncertainty avoidance (UA)	Problemistic search (PS)	Organizational learning (OL)
Strategic flexibility (SF)	Meeting and interview data	4	7	16	39
	Company documents	2	2	2	15
Fixed asset parsimony leveraged intellectual assets (FAP)	Meeting and interview data	1	1	5	59
	Company documents	0	1	2	35
Coordination through modular product architecture (MPA)	Meeting and interview data	0	0	0	0
	Company documents	0	0	0	0

Table 4.15 Decision-making concepts and text references

	Quasi resolution of conflict (RoC)	Uncertainty avoidance (UA)	Problemistic search (PS)	Organizational learning (OL)
Meeting and interview data	99	161	480	649
Company documents	23	14	52	202

Table 4.16 Central strategy concepts and text references

	Strategic flexibility (SF)	Fixed asset parsimony (FAP)	Modular product architecture (MPA)
Meeting and interview data	328	74	3
Company documents	92	40	0

such the idea of developing a machine 'guardian' at WYM is a prime example where a person will be dedicated in each area to be the area's machine expert holding the specialized knowledge and becoming a point of reference for the specific machine:

"We hand it to a designated operator here who is the machine guardian".

In the human resources manual, there is an emphasis in staff development and learning:

> "WYM believes in fair treatment to all employees by providing training and giving the appropriate knowledge so staff can live up to expectations and deliver great work", and
>
> "Employee involvement is a process for empowering members of the organization to make decisions and solve problems appropriately to their level in the organization. The basis of employee involvement is to align power, knowledge and information to providing superior customer value".

In the product development manual, there is learning and strategic flexibility displayed in the following example. In this text excerpt WYM presents some factors that need careful consideration when developing new products:

> "Understanding user needs, strategic alignment, regulation compliance, product channel and support, product endorsement by upper management".

In the business plan document emphasis is given on building a technically competent staff base that can respond to market opportunities:

> "Building a staff base that is technically competent, has a 'can do' attitude, are flexible in approach and enthusiastic", and
>
> "The growth potential of the current products and their fit with bigger volume carpet makers (broadloom operations) is a major identified market opportunity. To prepare for the predicted growth period, we need to be developing superior processing machinery that gives a product the consistency expected in broadloom operations, to retain current customers and stimulate repeat orders by marketing products that are specific for our customers and their market segment. A major component of implementing the plan relies on continuing to building excellent relationships with all agents and sector customers. Controls in place are geared towards the objectives with reporting and monitoring by members of the management team being focused to improving delivery schedules and general business practices including product quality monitoring and improvements".

How decision-making processes affect central strategy processes at WYM

Across all central strategy processes at WYM the most commonly occurring relationships are between fixed asset parsimony and the organizational learning concept of decision-making (see Table 4.14). The role of learning is also evidenced within the strategic flexibility concept.

The total count of common text references between decision-making and central strategy constructs (the rows in yellow in Table 4.14) is 132. From this, 50 per cent of references indicate evidence of fixed asset parsimony approach within the decision-making concepts and more specific in the organizational learning concept of decision-making. The concept of strategic flexibility also has a strong relationship to the decision-making concepts as evidenced in the remaining 50 per cent of the common references. There is no relationship between decision-making and modular product architecture concepts. The role of learning is also evidenced in the findings from the document analysis however the remaining findings from the document analysis are minimal or non-existent.

More specific the role of learning in fixed asset parsimony is evidenced when improving firm processes. The role of decision-making in the strategic flexibility concept is also evidenced when improving firm processes, when enhancing technology or when maintaining a competitive advantage. However, the concept of modular product architecture is non-existent at WYM.

RQ2a product creation and business sustainability outcomes

The product creation construct as previously seen encapsulates two theoretical concepts, real-time market research (RTMR) and multiple firm collaborations (MC). Through linking RTMR to the business sustainability outcomes of environmental (EnvS), financial (FinS) and social sustainability (SocS) there is indicative evidence that customer expectations or challenging customer behaviours or various quality issues surrounding the incoming raw wool sliver can have a negative impact on the financial position of the firm. Additionally, WYM is keen to investigate new market opportunities as and when they arise to improve their financial position. However, the concept of multiple firm collaborations (MC) was found to have no influence on any of the business sustainability outcomes.

Figure 4.10 displays the concept map generated for product creation and business sustainability outcomes, with all concepts and compounded concepts. Figure 4.11 displays all themes. The 'hottest' theme appearing in red is *real-time market research*.

In Figure 4.12, we display all concepts and compounded ones for product creation and business sustainability outcomes in descending count order. Two compounded concepts are missing as they have zero common text references. These are (a) *multiple collaborations* and *environmental sustainability*, and (b) *multiple collaborations* and *social sustainability*. As previously seen in answering RQ1a, RTMR is the highest-ranked concept among the product creation concepts in section. When linked to the FinS the co-occurrence of these two concepts is evidenced in forty-four text references indicating that the financial position of the firm is influenced through the real-time research market concept.

We proceed by presenting the results in a tabular form. Table 4.17 displays common text between product creation and business sustainability concepts. The rows represent the product creation and columns the business sustainability concepts. Tables 4.18 and 4.19 represent the individual text references for each concept. The financial sustainability (FinS) concept scores the highest among the

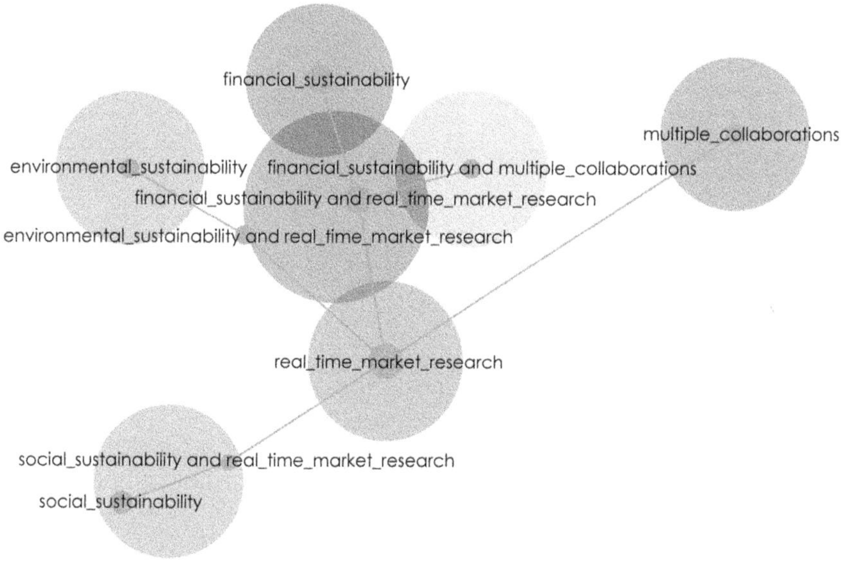

Figure 4.10 Concept map for product creation and business sustainability outcomes

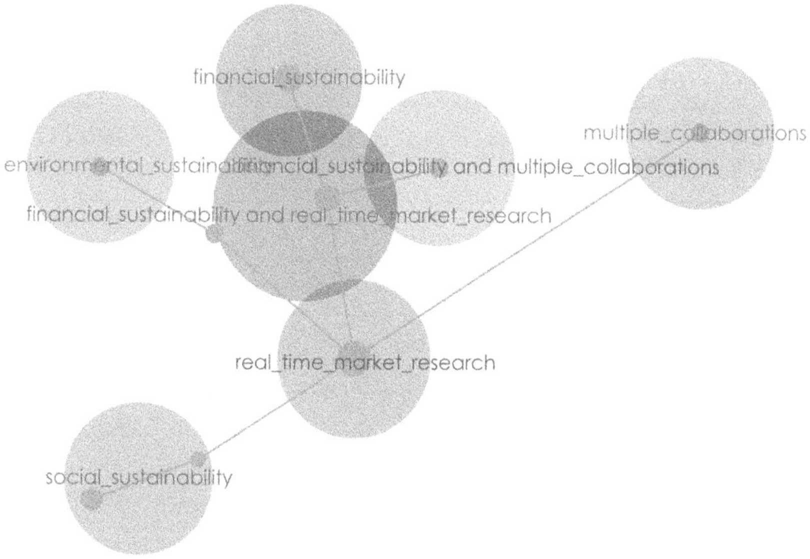

Figure 4.11 Themes map for product creation and business sustainability outcomes

Word-Like	Count	Relevance	
real_time_market_research	842	100%	
financial_sustainability	204	24%	
multiple_collaborations	166	20%	
environmental_sustainability	49	06%	
financial_sustainability and real_time_market_research	44	05%	
social_sustainability	13	02%	
environmental_sustainability and real_time_market_research	10	01%	
financial_sustainability and multiple_collaborations	4	00%	
social_sustainability and real_time_market_research	3	00%	

Figure 4.12 Concepts for product creation and business sustainability outcomes

Table 4.17 Product creation and business sustainability outcomes

	Environmental sustainability (EnvS)	Financial sustainability (FinS)	Social sustainability (SocS)
Real-time market research (RTMR)	10	44	3
Multiple short-term collaborations (MC)	0	4	0

Table 4.18 Product creation concepts with count of text references

Real-time market research (RTMR)	*Multiple short-term collaborations (MC)*
842	166

Table 4.19 Business sustainability outcomes with count of text references

Environmental sustainability (EnvS)	*Financial sustainability (FinS)*	*Social sustainability (SocS)*
49	204	13

business sustainability outcomes with 204 text references. That is indicative of a firm that strives to optimize their financial position. Among the highest-ranked synonyms are money (102), sales (sixty), financial (twenty-two) and cash flow (sixteen).

The following examples are from debriefing meetings that the general manager gave to the staff at various points in time encouraging them to be financially sustainable:

> "If we can clear it and get some money for it that is the only thing we can do", and
>
> "We have got to survive and make money if we got to be there and service them".

Synonyms such as sales, financial and cash flow *also promote financial sustainability thinking as seen from the following examples:*

> "It is not a contract but it is basically saying how and what we should expect from each other. They will say that they expect a sales forecast from us and I say yes but it is a non-binding sales forecast", and
>
> "He suggests that they need to have a review on stock because he wants to kill all redundant stock by the end of the **financial** year", and
>
> "Just to make a comment there, most of these assets the investment has been made out of **cash flow** which needs closely monitoring".

Real-time market research and sustainable outcomes

The concept of real-time market research (RTMR) is most commonly evidenced within the financial sustainability outcomes of the company. Through a systematic analysis of the common text excerpts we defined and presented next empirically derived concepts where evidence of the co-occurrence of theoretical concepts existed within my data set.

Dealing with customer behaviours

WYM carefully sets the product prices when new customer orders come through as the following example indicates:

> "Also they talked about a customer L and a quote that they gave about 6 weeks ago but this is well out of date now because the price is changed by now so they need to quote the new price now".

Some customers present challenges to the management of WYM. That said, this customer is the exception rather than the norm and refuses to pay the full amount for various reasons. WYM must carefully handle situations like these:

> "Today there was an issue from a customer B to whom there is a container shipment due out of NZ tomorrow but there is no payment or confirmation of payment received and George refuses point blank to let the container leave

without any money. The problem with that is that if the container does not leave (as a result of customer B not having paid) it means that WYM has to put it in a space at WYM which they don't have or pay out of their pockets to store it somewhere and wait for the next shipment or wait till the money have arrived from customer B", and

"He has restructured the whole business and the company that we were dealing before that does not exist anymore. D & B basically saying that you can put a shot across their belly and request that money and then they are basically happy to follow that up but it could be some hard work to get that".

In some instances, the supplied raw wool sliver falls short of the high standards required for further processing. It also ends up costing WYM a lot of time and money to bring it up to the standard required to process it:

"So all that this is reinforcing is that if we have a customer supplied product that it is not up to product spec we just give it back and say we are not prepared to run it. Even if we lose time at gilling even if we process some of it, it is not worth us wasting 3 times more because it is losing us money and you are going to carry on losing money through the whole process and worse than that it increases our lead time and we are off the beat".

In the following example, a customer feedback is influencing the financial position of the company. In this case, the product developed at WYM appeared to have shown some contamination (a red streaking in it) when shipped to the customer. WYM investigates the matter further and looks for ways to rectify the issue:

"At this point Paul enters the room and Caroline says to him that she has some photos that she needs to let him have a look at because they came from a client and they have red grease streaking in them. That grease appears in about 50 kilos of yarn which is quite worrying, how did that happen? George reckons that the client sent these photos to WYM so they can get some insurance money out of them".

Investigating market opportunities to improve financial position

Prices for raw materials fluctuate depending on market conditions. At times, they are high enough to force the management at WYM to consider other sources for securing the much-needed wool sliver:

"When I look at the latest price they just given us for just the fibre alone – we can get the fibre supplied through supplier S and if it is spun in supplier S it comes to us at a price of $5.40 because they are buying for the whole year".

They also investigate where market opportunities are and how they can exploit them. At the same time the economic downturn that affected most markets at the back end of 2008 is also affecting WYM generating a lot of uncertainty:

"So there is a lot of opportunities and most of our growth is coming from exist-ing customers that are seen increase in sales and the type of product that we are providing them it is not just going out and having a hunting approach we are keeping pretty much with people that we have got established products", and

"we are a little bit **uncertain** where we are in the growth curve. That is from a marketing perspective where is that actually heading on but potentially we still feel that is very early on and some of these growth curves will keep increasing", and

"At the moment over the last two months we have seen a drop of receipt of orders of less than 5 tonne a week, but saying that the two main factors on that is that European and the US markets and obviously the currency **uncer-tainties** so I don't know if that stops people to place orders at the moment. We have got a strong indication of forward sales pretty much by a big range of our customers but also making sure the stuff that we have got in the local market with the frieze and the Tussore products that we do for customer C".

WYM has carved a niche product market which is shown by the continuous cus-tomer demand, particularly from those customers termed as 'A' list or prime customers who place orders on a regular basis:

"There is not much to say much about the sales and marketing other than that the opportunity to sell depends on our ability to make and I think that is going to stay that way for the foreseeable future. General market condi-tions are very flat in Australia Europe etc. so we are in a very sweet spot and hopefully we will stay like that", and

"The opportunity to increase sales is still there I have to say that in terms of environment Europe is very flat and I don't see any changes in that for the foreseeable future. In the US I believe we have opportunities for further growth particularly among the A list people, people that we have identified as being of a good potential".

Multiple firm collaborations and sustainable outcomes

Although the concept of multiple firm collaborations (MC) on its own was evi-denced in 166 text references, there is no evidence to link MC to sustainable business outcomes. Hence, we conclude that MC had no impact on business sustainability outcomes at WYM.

Company document analysis

The findings from the meeting/interview data are compared with the findings from the document analysis data. Tables 4.20, 4.21 and 4.22 provide common text references as well as individual concept text count.

Table 4.20 Product creation and business sustainability outcomes

		Environmental sustainability (EnvS)	Financial sustainability (FinS)	Social sustainability (SocS)
Real-time market research (RTMR)	Meeting and interview data	10	44	3
	Company documents	8	28	5
Multiple short-term collaborations (MC)	Meeting and interview data	0	4	0
	Company documents	0	2	0

Table 4.21 Product creation concepts with count of text references

	Real-time market research (RTMR)	Multiple short-term collaborations (MC)
Meeting and interview data	842	166
Company documents	398	31

Table 4.22 Business sustainability outcomes with count of text references

	Environmental sustainability (EnvS)	Financial sustainability (FinS)	Social sustainability (SocS)
Meeting and interview data	49	204	13
Company documents	106	60	12

There is evidence that environmental sustainability, at least on paper, existed in the case study organization. The environmental sustainability (EnvS) concept was identified in 106 text references. However, when linked to product creation concepts it did not yield similar results. What follows are some text references where EnvS is apparent. These examples demonstrate a continuous commitment to environmental improvements:

> "WYM is committed to continual improvement of its environmental performance. This includes a commitment to promoting sustainable environmental management, internally (employees) and externally (contractors, visitors, and the general public) to prevent and/or reduce pollution and increase resource efficiency", and
>
> "WYM will dispose of residues (residual management) in an environmentally safe way. We believe the environmental management is a responsibility of every person on site", and

"We will establish guidelines and annual targets to achieve efficient use of renewable and non-renewable resources relative to the site s activities. WYM is committed to accurately recording and reporting, regularly monitoring, and annually auditing environmental performance", and

"Take all practicable steps to ensure environmental protection and minimum impact while at work. Follow supervisor's instructions. Use and look after all equipment provided", and

"Audits are carried out by the environmental management representative and management", and

"No worker is expected to work unsupervised in an area in which they have not been trained", and

"The environmental management system objectives and targets are reviewed annually signed by the manager responsible for achieving the objectives/target at each function and level of the organization. The timeframe for each objective/target is specified".

RTMR is also evidenced within business sustainability outcomes as shown in the following examples:

"If you think like your customer, then you would put yourself in your customer shoes. Before we set any policy, before we spent any money, before we make any decisions, before we take any action, before we even opened our mouth, we would ask ourselves, If I was the customer, what would I want to see happen?" and

"Active and effective product development programme measures the number of products that make it to prime status (commercial volume and revenue). Feedback from customer base ensures customer satisfaction", and

"By using the stage gate process it is expected to promote products that will reach prime status (regular volume sales with premium contribution margin) and to nip in the bud ideas that cannot be supported by a business case", and

"There is a strong awareness about market and industry changes that are occurring and the impact they can have on WYM business sales and operations. WYM is actively engaged in further product developments to keep current and ensuring very good service levels".

How product creation affect business sustainability outcomes

The total count of common text references (in Table 4.20) is sixty-one. In contrast to previous research questions, there are far less evidence that links product creation processes to the business sustainability outcomes. From the overall sixty-one common text references a 93 per cent of this refers to the theoretical concept of real-time market research links to the business sustainability outcomes. That said the concept is mostly evidenced around the environmental and financial elements of sustainability when dealing with customers' behaviours or when investigating market opportunities further.

For the other product creation concept of multiple collaborations there is no apparent contribution on the business sustainability outcomes. The conclusion is that real-time market research is the only product creation concept which partially affects any sustainable outcomes. A similar pattern occurs in findings from the document analysis.

RQ2b product strategy and business sustainability outcomes

The product strategy construct as previously seen encapsulates the theoretical concepts, speed to market (S2M), rapid performance upgrade through improved components (RPU) and proliferation of product variety (PPV). When we link S2M with the business sustainability concepts we observed indicative evidence that the firm strives for technology or production process improvements to increase production efficiencies.

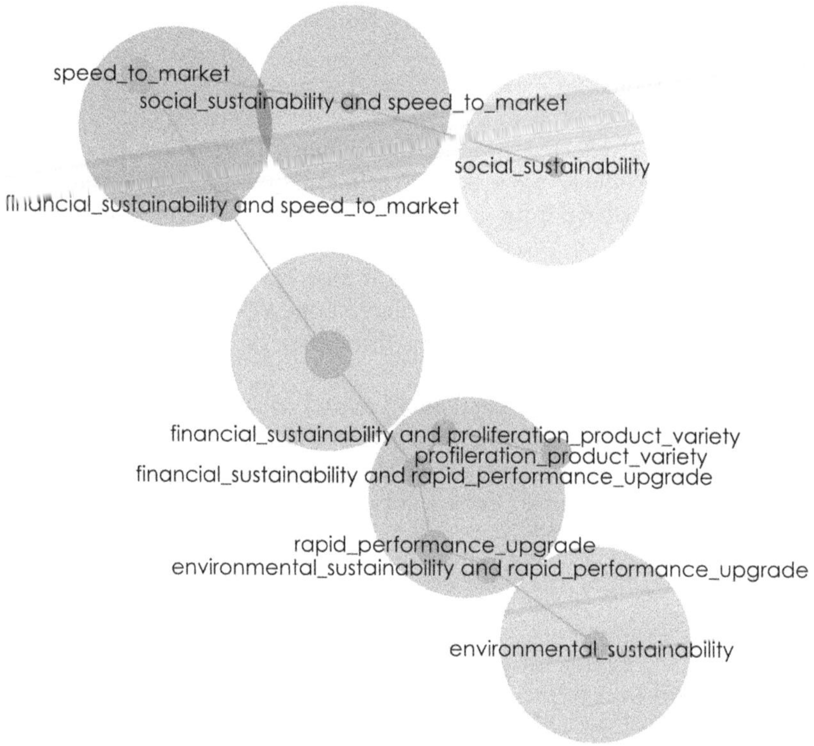

speed_to_market
social_sustainability and speed_to_market
social_sustainability
financial_sustainability and speed_to_market

financial_sustainability and proliferation_product_variety
profileration_product_variety
financial_sustainability and rapid_performance_upgrade

rapid_performance_upgrade
environmental_sustainability and rapid_performance_upgrade

environmental_sustainability

Figure 4.13 Concept map for product strategy and business sustainability outcomes

However, when we link the remaining two concepts (RPU) and (PPV) to the business sustainability outcomes there is minimal or non-existent evidence that these concepts affect the environmental, financial or social performance of WYM.

Figure 4.13 displays the concept map generated for product strategy and business sustainability outcomes with all concepts and compounded concepts. Figure 4.14 displays all themes. The 'hottest' theme (in red) is *rapid performance upgrade*. However, there is a potential confusion of the 'hottest' theme being *rapid performance upgrade* and yet there is no evidence to link RPU to business sustainability outcomes. Earlier, we noted that for this study we used the default theme size of 33 per cent allowing Leximancer to cluster concepts according to the 33 per cent. Hence with 33 per cent theme visibility, Leximancer has clustered the most concepts in theme *rapid performance upgrade*. Indeed, the reader notices in Figure 4.13 that this theme contains two concepts *(proliferation of product variety and rapid performance upgrade)* and three compounded concepts *(financial sustainability and proliferation of product variety, financial sustainability and rapid performance upgrade and environmental sustainability*

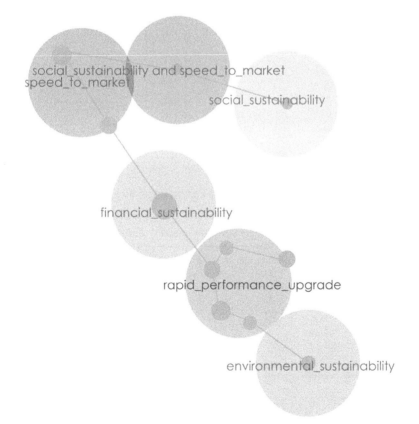

Figure 4.14 Themes map for product strategy and business sustainability outcomes

and rapid performance upgrade) more than any other theme. All five concepts appear together often in the same pieces of text and for this reason they attract one another strongly, and tend to settle near one another in the map space. Therefore because this theme has the most concepts it is heat-mapped as the 'hottest'.

Figure 4.15 displays all concepts and compounded ones for product strategy and business sustainability outcomes in descending count order. Four pairs have no common text references and are hence omitted from the Figure 4.15. These are (a) *speed to market* and *environmental sustainability*, (b) *rapid performance upgrade* and *social sustainability*, (c) *proliferation of product variety* and *environmental sustainability* and (d) *proliferation of product variety* and *social sustainability*.

We then present the results in a tabular form. Table 4.23 displays common text between product strategy and business sustainability concepts. The rows

Word-Like	Count	Relevance	
speed_to_market	451	100%	
financial_sustainability	204	45%	
rapid_performance_upgrade	161	36%	
proliferation_product_variety	131	29%	
environmental_sustainability	49	11%	
financial_sustainability and speed_to_market	15	03%	
social_sustainability	13	03%	
financial_sustainability and rapid_performance_upgrade	8	02%	
financial_sustainability and proliferation_product_variety	7	02%	
environmental_sustainability and rapid_performance_upgrade	3	01%	
social_sustainability and speed_to_market	1	00%	

Figure 4.15 Concepts for product strategy and business sustainability outcomes

Table 4.23 Product strategy and business sustainability outcomes

	Environmental sustainability (EnvS)	Financial sustainability (FinS)	Social sustainability (SocS)
Speed to market (S2M)	0	15	1
Rapid performance upgrade through improved components (RPU)	3	8	0
Proliferation of product variety (PPV)	0	7	0

Table 4.24 Product strategy concepts with count of text references

Speed to market (S2M)	Rapid performance upgrade (RPU)	Proliferation product variety (PPV)
451	161	131

Table 4.25 Business sustainability outcomes with count of text references

Environmental sustainability (EnvS)	Financial sustainability (FinS)	Social sustainability (SocS)
49	204	13

represent the product strategy and columns the business sustainability concepts. Tables 4.24 and 4.25 represent the individual text references for each concept.

The findings show some links between product strategy concepts and business sustainability outcomes which are explained further in the following sections.

Speed to market and sustainable outcomes

Speed to market is the highest scoring concept among the product strategy concepts with 451 text references. The concept is mostly evidenced together with the financial performance at WYM and it is related to technology and production process improvements at WYM. In the next sections, we present two empirically derived concepts that emerge from the intersection of S2M with sustainable business outcomes.

Improve technology

Machinery upgrades, or acquisitions may reduce the time needed to develop products. More specifically it can improve the time spent to develop products, which subsequently impacts on the financial aspect of sustainability:

> "The machines can be converted with substantial money but the payback is quick and if WYM wants to ride the wave they need to have the appropriate machinery".

The ability to improve on the speed in which product reach customer is very important as that will maintain customer loyalty. Sometimes customers are prepared to airfreight products to save up on times that would otherwise require if shipped:

> "They cannot afford to have 12 or 13 weeks lead time because customers will be disheartened and go elsewhere", and
> "They are out of stock on that particular yarn and he wants this one to get out of RYT to them as soon as possible possibly by airfreight

as Caroline point out they have a very good price on express so they can do it like that".

Speed to market is an important key performance indicator. That said the general manager is concerned that if staff constantly work over and above what is required, that will have a negative impact on their health:

> "George says that we can do that in our current structure but he doesn't want to see people basting 50 hour weeks because they will get too tired and can't do anything after that and it is not sustainable".

Improve process

At times concerns were raised around the quality of the incoming raw sliver which was below the standard required. WYM was firm not to accept any sub-standard product and indicated that firmly to the supplier:

> "So all that this is reinforcing is that if we have a customer supplied product that it is not up to product spec we just give it back and say we are not prepared to run it. Even if we lose time at gilling even if we process some of it, it is not worth us wasting 3 times more because it is losing us money and you are going to carry on losing money through the whole process and worse than that it increases our lead time".

Rapid performance upgrade and sustainable outcomes

The concept of rapid performance upgrade through technology components (RPU) is not evidenced clearly within business sustainability outcomes. The limited findings do not add value to this study. Hence, we conclude that RPU does not affect any sustainable aspects within the case study organization.

However, despite that the RPU concept did not impact upon sustainable business outcomes, it is important to note that a company a company who continuously improves their assets (i.e. machinery, human capabilities) also reap financial benefits in the long-term. Among the technology improvements that significantly impacted on the quality of the finished product include a new production machine for their specialty yarn which increased production and helped minimize lead times. In addition, extra gilling capacity to alleviate the demand pressure of the gills was implemented during my data collection phase at WYM. Various machinery upgrades in the roving area, and the 'tower' cans project all resulted in higher quantities of yarn being produced and dried again helping to decrease lead times and effectively improving the financial performance of the firm.

Proliferation of product variety and sustainable outcomes

The concept of proliferation of product variety (PPV) is not clearly evidenced within the business sustainability outcomes. It is however important to note here that good business practices were shepherded by the general manager to develop a small number of new products at any one time. That way the product feedback happens quicker and hence the product commercialization and financial performance is accelerated:

> "So I don't see value going into other product developments, if our table has got more than 10 then we need to decide who are our top 10, that is my approach to it", and
> "As opposed to have lots of product developments in nurture, but once we choose to commercialise them then we can put some focus to production. At the moment we are still picking up a lot of customer driven thoughts and it might make money for them but is it going to make money for us?"

Company document analysis

The findings from the meeting and interview data are compared with the findings from the document analysis data. Tables 4.26, 4.27 and 4.28 provide common text references as well as individual concept text count. The lack of common text references in the document analysis led us to conclude that the product strategy concepts did not affect in any way business sustainability outcomes.

How product strategy affect business sustainability outcomes

The findings indicate that the product strategy concepts have limited impact on the sustainability outcomes. There are thirty-four common references between the two constructs in Table 4.26. From all three product strategy concepts speed to market is moderately linked to the business sustainability outcomes with sixteen common references (47 per cent of total references) and moreover

Table 4.26 Product strategy and business sustainability outcomes

		Environmental sustainability (EnvS)	Financial sustainability (FinS)	Social sustainability (SocS)
Speed to market (S2M)	Meeting and interview data	0	15	1
	Company documents	0	4	0
Rapid performance upgrade through improved components (RPU)	Meeting and interview data	3	8	0
	Company documents	2	2	0
Proliferation of product variety (PPV)	Meeting and interview data	0	7	0
	Company documents	0	0	0

Table 4.27 Product Strategy concepts with count of text references

	Speed to market (S2M)	Rapid performance upgrade (RPU)	Proliferation product variety (PPV)
Meeting and interview data	451	161	131
Company documents	46	34	7

Table 4.28 Business sustainability outcomes with count of text references

	Environmental sustainability (EnvS)	Financial sustainability (FinS)	Social sustainability (SocS)
Meeting and interview data	49	204	13
Company documents	106	60	12

it is the only one that impacts upon the financial performance of the company. The findings from the document analysis are far lower (eight references in total) however they show a similar pattern to the findings from the meetings, interviews and observations.

More specific speed to market and financial sustainability is mostly evidenced when technology or production process improvements take place. There is no clear evidence that the two remaining concepts of rapid performance upgrade and proliferation of product variety impact upon business sustainability outcomes.

RQ2c central strategy and business sustainability outcomes

The central strategy construct encapsulates the theoretical concepts, strategic flexibility (SF), fixed asset parsimony (FAP) and modular product architecture (MPA). The findings indicate that a strategic flexibility approach enables WYM to minimize their environmental impact and optimize their financial performance. There are no links between the remaining central strategy concepts and the business sustainability outcomes. Hence, we conclude that both fixed asset parsimony and modular product architecture has no impact upon any sustainable business outcomes.

Figure 4.16 displays the concept map generated for *central strategy processes and business sustainability outcomes* with all concepts and compounded concepts. Figure 4.17 displays all themes. The 'hottest' theme is *environmental sustainability*.

Figure 4.18 displays the concepts and all compound concepts in descending count order. Strategic flexibility concept scores the highest among the central strategy concepts with 328 text references.

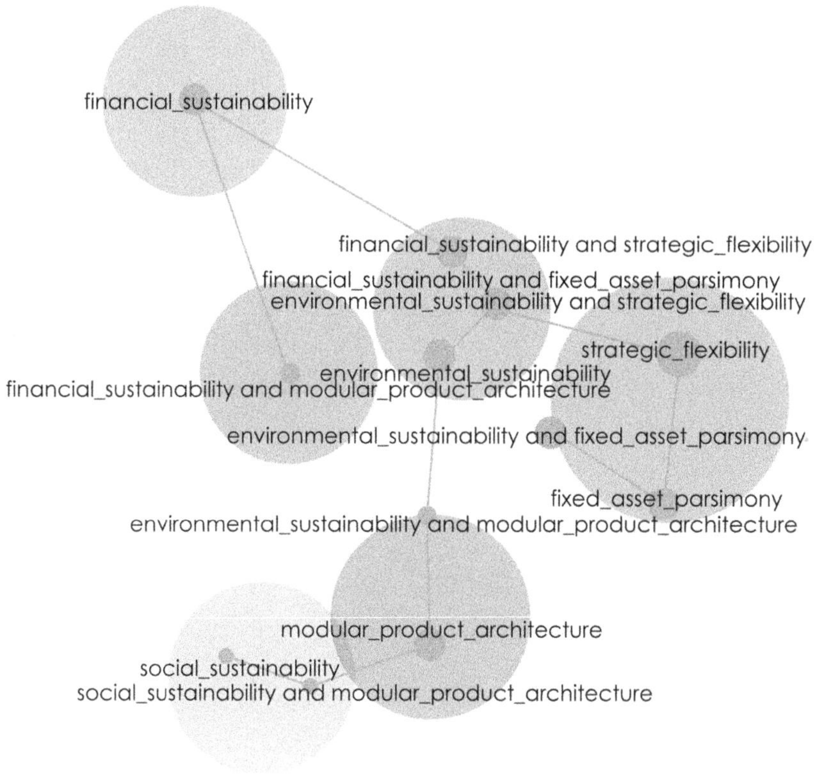

Figure 4.16 Concept map for central strategy processes and business sustainability
outcomes

Table 4.29 displays common text between central strategy and business sustainability concepts. The rows represent the central strategy and columns the
business sustainability concepts. Tables 4.30 and 4.31 present the individual text
references for each concept.

In the following sections, we further examine the links between strategic flexibility approach and environmental and financial sustainable outcomes.

Strategic flexibility and sustainable business outcomes

The strategic flexibility (SF) concept of central strategy links to the financial outcome
of sustainability with eight common references and to the environmental sustainability with six common references. Strategic flexibility and environmental awareness is
witnessed in the 'competitive manufacturing' initiative that took part at WYM:

> "The strategy George wants to apply is for the staff to start using competitive
> manufacturing and then seeding the idea but then we need to start thinking

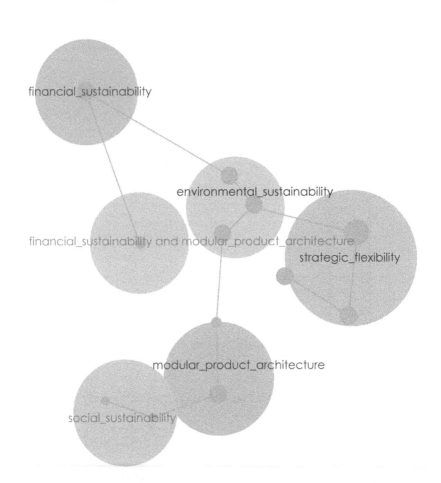

Figure 4.17 Themes map for central strategy processes and business sustainability outcomes

Word-Like	Count	Relevance	
strategic_flexibility	328	100%	
financial_sustainability	204	62%	
fixed_asset_parsimony	74	23%	
modular_product_architecture	67	20%	
environmental_sustainability	49	15%	
social_sustainability	13	04%	
financial_sustainability and strategic_flexibility	8	02%	
environmental_sustainability and strategic_flexibility	6	02%	
environmental_sustainability and modular_product_architecture	2	01%	
environmental_sustainability and fixed_asset_parsimony	2	01%	
financial_sustainability and fixed_asset_parsimony	1	00%	
social_sustainability and modular_product_architecture	1	00%	
financial_sustainability and modular_product_architecture	1	00%	

Figure 4.18 Concepts for central strategy processes and business sustainability outcomes

Table 4.29 Central strategy and business sustainability outcomes

	Minimize environmental impact (E)	Optimize financial performance (F)	Optimize social effect (S)
Strategic flexibility (SF)	6	8	0
Fixed asset parsimony leveraged intellectual assets (FAP)	2	1	0
Coordination through modular product architecture (MPA)	2	0	0

Table 4.30 Central strategy concepts with count of text references

Strategic flexibility (SF)	Fixed asset parsimony (FAP)	Modular product architecture (MPA)
328	74	3

Table 4.31 Business sustainability outcomes with count of text references

Environmental sustainability (EnvS)	Financial sustainability (FinS)	Social sustainability (SocS)
49	204	13

of what things to measure and what we will measure is how we reduce operating costs by using less energy and making sure we use our components
very well", and

"Because if they are competitive at manufacturing they will be profitable
and the goal is business excellence in that area and along the way you are
dragging along quality, health and safety and also dragging along good environmental impacts because that is part of the thinking".

Strategic flexibility and financial sustainability outcome is reflected in the firm's
ability to develop both flexible resources (i.e. increase the range of alternative
uses to which machinery can be applied) and cognitive flexibilities of the staff.
During the meetings, they discussed machinery upgrades or acquisitions, which
was an indication of crafting a strategic plan to allow them to process an increasing number of customer orders:

"Talking about the importance of getting the machine upgraded . . . orders
are coming thick and fast . . . we will start losing customers".

In addition, some operational changes like increasing the business hours to eighteen hours daily (from sixteen hours previously), to working the roving areas on a twenty-four hour, five-day schedule for the short term, to employing more staff or to delivering products to the customer fast and reflecting that to the price charged to the customer, are all signs of anticipating future product demand and handling it by exhibiting a strategic flexibility approach.

At times of heightened product demand which inflicted high stress on existing resources, a board member indicated the need to examine the profitability of customers. According to the same member when the company sold product development capacity, they still assessed it regarding product, and he argued that they should assess it on customer by customer criteria:

> "We need to be doing customer profitability profiles and product profitability profiles within customers".

Finally, strategic flexibility was prominent when WYM involved themselves in discussions with a sheep breeders group to secure a sustainable supply chain of locally sourced raw wool. Having already achieved a competitive advantage with their innovative technology, WYM aimed to build on that by developing this partnership between themselves and the wool supplier.

Company document analysis

The findings from the meetings and interview data are compared with the findings from the document analysis data. Tables 4.32, 4.33 and 4.34 provide common text references as well as individual concept text count.

Table 4.32 Central strategy and business sustainability outcomes

		Minimize environmental impact (E)	Optimize financial performance (F)	Optimize social effect (S)
Strategic flexibility (SF)	Meeting and interview data	6	8	0
	Company documents	1	10	1
Fixed asset parsimony leveraged intellectual assets (FAP)	Meeting and interview data	2	1	0
	Company documents	0	0	0
Coordination through modular product architecture (MPA)	Meeting and interview data	2	0	0
	Company documents	0	0	0

Table 4.33 Central strategy concepts with count of text references

	Strategic flexibility (SF)	Fixed asset parsimony (FAP)	Modular product architecture (MPA)
Meeting and interview data	328	74	3
Company documents	92	40	0

Table 4.34 Business sustainability outcomes with count of text references

	Environmental sustainability (EnvS)	Financial sustainability (FinS)	Social sustainability (SocS)
Meeting and interview data	49	204	13
Company documents	106	60	12

The findings on paper present some evidence of strategic flexibility approach to optimize the financial performance of the company as presented in the following examples:

> "Speed yields higher profitability. The revenue from sales of the product is realised earlier and the revenues over the life of the product are higher given a fixed window of opportunity and hence limited product life".
>
> "Rug and Carpet yarn has been a star growth item. This is relevant, as WYM have been able to increase sales without directly taking sales from competitors".
>
> "By monitoring unit sales and dollar sales to different locations of New Zealand a broad picture can be obtained. Personal contact with customers about two times a year is also required to observe market changes and marketplace (rug/carpet makers) reactions".
>
> "Building a staff base that is technically competent has a 'can do' attitude, are flexible and enthusiastic".

How central strategy affect business sustainability outcomes

The total count of common text references in Table 4.32 is nineteen.

As with previous research questions, there is far less evidence that links central strategy processes to the business sustainability outcomes. From the nineteen overall common text references more than half amounting to fourteen references were found linking the strategic flexibility theoretical concept to the environmental and financial elements of sustainability. This meant that there is a strong relationship of 73 per cent between strategic flexibility and business sustainability outcomes. However, for the remaining two central strategy concepts the evidence of links with business sustainability outcomes is unclear. A similar pattern is encountered in findings from the document analysis.

Summary of the main findings

This section presents the main findings from systematically analyzing the data collected at the case study organization and provides answers to the research questions for this thesis. The way we preceded at first was to disaggregate each research question to its basic constructs and search for links in the form of common text references among concepts. We then systematically analyzed these links and derived a range of empirical concepts. We also sought to rate the relationships among the various theoretical concepts as strong (50 per cent or above), moderate (20 per cent to 49 per cent) or weak (19 per cent or less), the percentage of which was calculated by comparing the number of common text references in a relationship to the overall count of common references of the two theoretical constructs that the relationship came out of.

Table 4.35 displays the empirical concepts found from answering the research questions. The rows represent the nine empirical concepts and the columns represent the six research questions. All rows apart from the first one, which we explain shortly, appear in descending order in terms of how many research questions each empirical concept addresses.

Overall the findings indicate that the decision-making concepts of organizational learning, uncertainty avoidance, problemistic search and quasi resolution of conflict are mostly evidenced in the product creation concept of real-time market research. Indeed, as shown previously (refer to section 4.1.5), a total of 332 references out of an overall 361 common references between decision-making and product creation constructs reflect the appearance of real-time market

Table 4.35 Empirical concepts

Research strand *Empirical concepts*	RQ1a	RQ1b	RQ1c	RQ2a	RQ2b	RQ2c
Learning from feedback	X					
Improving process		X	X		X	X
Improving technology		X	X		X	X
Dealing with customer behaviours	X	X		X		
Harness market opportunities	X	X		X		
Maintain a competitive advantage			X			X
Uncertainty in development	X					
Problem solving and learning through collaborations	X					
Mitigating supply chain uncertainties	X					

research within the decision-making processes. Drilling further into these 332 references, there is an overwhelming majority (236 references) linking real-time market research to organizational learning. This strong relationship between the two theoretical concepts is the reason we chose to define the empirical concept of *learning from feedback*.

However organizational learning is not only evidenced in research question RQ1a. We draw the attention of the reader to sections 4.2.1.3 dealing with technology improvements, 4.2.2.1 improving the drying process of the yarn with the 'tower cans', 4.2.3 seeking to resolve some operational issues around product development, 4.3.2.1 dealing with issues surrounding poor quality of raw wool and 4.3.4 discussing the idea of a machine 'guardian' at WYM. Enhanced learning is exhibited in all these activities hence this theoretical concept is also implicitly addressed in research questions RQ1b and RQ1c. Furthermore, when analyzing the findings for the remaining research questions there is an underlying presence of learning implied from past experiences in dealing with customers (RQ2a), or when speed to market is concerned (RQ2b), or when the 'competitive manufacturing' business initiative was implemented. For that reason, we conclude that the theoretical concept of organizational learning is evidenced in all research questions.

Following on from 'learning from feedback', another two empirical concepts where also highly evidenced among the findings: *improve technology* and *improve processes*. More specific WYM's management team were constantly up against increasing 'lead' times. Trying to keep the 'lead' times to a minimum was reflected in the company's efforts to optimize production processes and improve technology and clearly evidenced in the findings of research question RQ1b. Maintaining a desirable level on 'lead' times, enabled the firm to enjoy some financial benefits evidenced in the findings of research question RQ2b. In addition to these research questions, the two empirical findings were also evidenced in RQ1c and RQ2c. In RQ1c the strategic flexibility approach that the management team adopted, commanded investing in upgrading machinery or acquiring new technology or seeking ways to improve production processes. In RQ2c the strategic flexibility approach enabled WYM to reap some financial and environmental benefits.

Dealing with customer behaviours is an empirical concept evidenced in research questions RQ1a, RQ1b and RQ2a. At times the customer behaviours were challenging and required careful handling by the management team. In other occasions the heightened customer demand was causing great concerns due to the limited production capacity. Hence the team was carefully planning and prioritizing jobs so they could be developed on time and to the customer expectation. Alternative shipping routes were often explored to increase speed in product deliveries.

How the firm *harnesses market opportunities* is another empirical concept observed in three research questions: RQ1a, RQ1b and RQ2a. WYM used feedback mechanisms to explore new market trends and product design opportunities so that they can develop niche products. As market conditions were often unstable (i.e. raw material price fluctuations, heightened customer demand, poor quality of incoming raw sliver), WYM explored alternative ways of sourcing raw materials, servicing demanding customers or improving quality of wool sliver. In doing so WYM also improved their financial position.

The empirical concept of *maintaining competitive advantage* is evident in two research questions: RQ1c and RQ2c. The findings indicate that WYM employed a strategic flexibility approach demonstrated in their ability to adapt to changing market conditions to remain competitive. That was evidenced in WYM's response to high customer demands, in seeking alternative supplier sources when raw material prices fluctuate and in designing and crafting products that most traditional spinners cannot do. To remain competitive the firm also engaged in discussions to collaborate with a sheep breeders group that could greatly benefit their supply chain and in a business initiative 'competitive manufacturing' which aimed at increasing production efficiencies and improve work spaces and staff morale.

The remaining three empirical concepts were mainly evidenced in research question RQ1a. These were:

1 *Uncertainty in development* – whether that is in product development or machinery upgrades and acquisitions is also another empirical concept clearly emerging from linking decision-making to product creation theoretical concepts.
2 *Problem solving and learning through collaborations* – is an approach to solve various issues and enhance firm's knowledge by embarking into collaborations with other firms.
3 *Mitigating supply chain uncertainties* – show how WYM responds to fluctuating market conditions previously discussed.

Table 4.36 presents a different way of looking at the findings. The rows indicate the common text references for each research question as well as the number of empirical concepts addressed in each question. RQ1a has the most common text references signifying that at WYM there is substantial evidence of decision-making processes within the product creation practices. There is also evidence of decision-making processes appearing within the product strategy and central strategy practices. However, there is limited evidence that product creation,

Table 4.36 Summary of the findings per research question

Research question	Total count of common references	Number of empirical concepts
RQ1a	361	6
RQ1b	140	4
RQ1c	132	3
RQ2a	61	2
RQ2b	34	2
RQ2c	19	3

product strategy or central strategy concepts impact mainly upon the financial aspect of business sustainability outcomes. There is no evidence of impact upon the social aspect of sustainable business outcomes at WYM.

Chapter summary

The aim of this chapter was to present the findings based on the analysis of the data collected at WYM. In doing so we first disaggregated each research question to its main constructs and concepts and sought links among the various theoretical concepts. We then systematically analyzed the findings which gave rise to nine empirical concepts some of them common to more than one research questions. We then answered the research questions and the chapter concluded with an identification of the main findings.

In the next chapter, we take the empirical concepts a step further and identify occurrences of these concepts in literature reviewed prior to answering my research questions. In addition, we seek further support validating the empirical concepts, from literature that we found after completing our fieldwork and analysis.

Notes

1 As the traditional cans posed a number of issues especially when heightened production times, a new improved version of the cans 'tower cans' was necessary to mitigate these issues. Tower cans are cylindrical drums that store yarn ready for drying. The name comes from a cylinder that is within the drum the 'tower'. The tower has numerous holes which allow hot air to circulate within the can and hence dry the yarn faster.
2 Usually one pass is sufficient for the majority of their products.
3 This is commonly referred to as Signed Order Confirmation (SOC) form.

Reference

Sanchez, R. (1995). Strategic flexibility in product competition. *Strategic Management Journal*, *16*, 135–159.

5 Theoretical perspectives on decision-making, new product development and sustainability in a small business

This chapter brings together the fieldwork through the findings presented in chapter four with the three bodies of literature examined in chapter two. In doing so this 'data-theory coupling' (Golden-Biddle and Locke, 2007, p. 52) looks into the forms and processes of organizational life encountered in the field. It also further evaluates the literature for similarities, differences or emerging patterns.

Effectively it partly fills the research space for the study encountered in the writing, through joining the worlds of the field and academy with the aim to 'theorize . . . fragments of life' (Golden-Biddle and Locke, 2007, p. 53) shown through the numerous data excerpts. We revisit the empirical concepts presented in chapter four in order of strength (the ones that are referenced in most questions down to the ones that have fewer references). For each concept, we cross reference the relevant literature from chapter two to provide theoretical support for my empirical findings. We seek further support from literature that we did not access in our original search, since the search for this additional literature has been guided by our empirical findings.

A revised theoretical framework: empirically derived concepts

We earlier defined a model that we termed 'sustainable product development decisions' which formed the basis of our original theoretical framework and enabled us to develop the research questions for this thesis. For ease of reading this model is presented here in Figure 5.1. In this theoretical framework, it was suggested that decision-making processes influenced concepts across product creation, product strategy, central strategy and business sustainability.

However, our findings paint a very different picture. Analysis of data gathered in meetings, interviews and through observations revealed no or limited evidence associated with many of the theoretical concepts defined in the original theoretical framework. Moreover, with respect to the limited number of theoretical concepts which had strong evidence associated with them, we found evidence of relationships between only a few of those concepts. These findings, based on interviews, meetings and observations, were further confirmed in analysis of company documents. When we further examined the various relationships among the

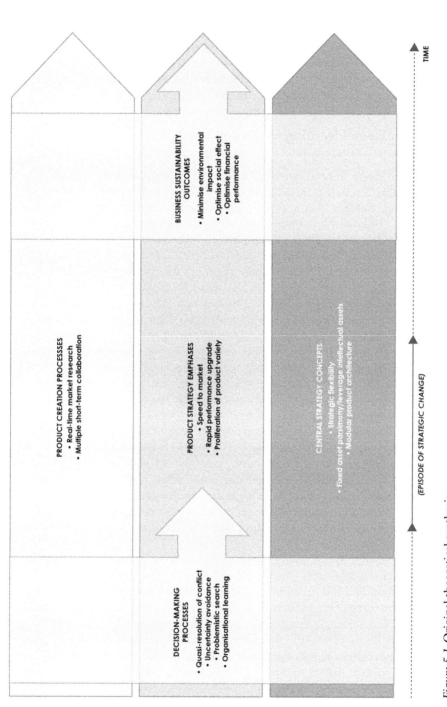

PRODUCT CREATION PROCESSSES
• Real-time market research
• Multiple short-term collaboration

BUSINESS SUSTAINABILITY OUTCOMES
• Minimise environmental impact
• Optimise social effect
• Optimise financial performance

PRODUCT STRATEGY EMPHASES
• Speed to market
• Rapid performance upgrade
• Proliferation of product variety

CENTRAL STRATEGY CONCEPTS
• Strategic flexibility
• Fixed asset parsimony/leverage intellectual assets
• Modular product architecture

DECISION-MAKING PROCESSES
• Quasi-resolution of conflict
• Uncertainty avoidance
• Problemistic search
• Organisational learning

(EPISODE OF STRATEGIC CHANGE)

TIME

Figure 5.1 Original theoretical synthesis

theoretical concepts of this framing, some appear to be strong, some moderate and some weak or non-existent (see section 4.7).

Hence, we revised our theoretical framework as shown in Figure 5.2. The intensity of the connecting lines reflects the quantity and quality of empirical support we found for the relationship each line defines. Subsequently, Figure 5.2 forms from now on the basis for the remainder of this discussion.

Organizational learning as the dominant decision-making process

By far the strongest relationship is between the organizational learning and real-time market research theoretical concepts which scored 91 per cent compared to the total number of concepts linking decision-making and product creation practices. Hence this is a clear indication that across all product creation processes WYM mostly apply feedback mechanisms incorporated in the theoretical concept of real-time research to enhance or generate new knowledge.

Across all product strategy processes at WYM the strongest relationship occurs between decision-making processes and speed to market which scored 50 per cent compared to the total number of concepts linking decision-making and product strategy. Of the four decision-making concepts, organizational learning is the one most commonly linked to speed to market.

Across all central strategy processes at WYM the role of learning is evidenced in two relationships: the relationship between organizational learning and fixed asset parsimony and the relationship between organizational learning and strategic flexibility. Indeed, these two relationships share the same weight with 50 per cent of common references in each one.

These findings further support and extend a body of empirical evidence which argues that organizational learning is a hugely important element (Cyert and March, 1992, pp. 161–176) in making and shaping organizational decisions. Learning from feedback is of significant value when new products are being developed since it assesses the performance of products and forecasts future demand portrayed through customers' satisfaction rates. Learning is also generated through technology improvements or new technology acquisitions as these create new knowledge.

We contend that our findings support the need for greater balance between a conventional marketing orientation and learning orientation. Being market-driven (Slater and Narver, 1995) enables firms to anticipate the developing needs of customers, bringing innovative products or services to them either 'just-in-time' or 'just-ahead' of changes in market preferences. At WYM, real-time market research was constantly used to learn more about market preferences and to improve market knowledge (Sanchez, 1996, p. 130). Our observations of WYM's real-time market research revealed a tension between ad hoc experimentation and a documented 'stage-gate' process (see section 3.3.4). Hence, we witnessed a cumulative process of trial and error, experimentation and search. This was interspersed with attempts to impose routines and learn from history. In

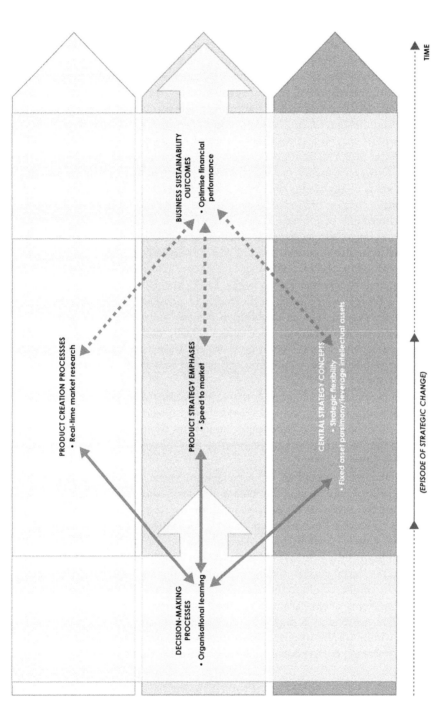

Figure 5.2 Revised theoretical synthesis

essence this might be conceptualized as 'learning by doing', which is essentially a process of performing limited changes to a product or a process, observing the consequences and refining the product or process in light of those consequences (Levitt and March, 1988, p. 321). However what became apparent was that the process was dependent on the manner in which customer feedback was gathered, and crucially, the attitude of the management team to that process (Caemmerer and Wilson, 2010) as revealed in the conflict between two of them the general manager and the director of R&D who was a co-owner.

This conflict may in fact be symptomatic of the evolution of different kinds of knowledge at WYM through a process of learning by doing (Sanchez, 1996, p. 136). However Sanchez (1996, p. 135) argues that different firms develop different kinds of knowledge that reflect different levels of understanding about their product creation processes: *know-how*, *know-why* and *know-what*. Each one of these three kinds of knowledge, provide a different strategic value to the company. For example, the *know-how* is all about the ability of the firm to produce and refine its existing product designs. There is certainly plenty of *know-how* at WYM surrounding the specialty yarn knowledge. *Know-why* is the 'theoretical understanding' of how the system works. In WYM this 'theoretical understanding' of the processes is reflected to the 'machine guardian' concept that the general manager was so keen to establish. *Know-why* knowledge enables the firm to adapt or develop a new product design. Finally *know-what* is the 'strategic understanding' of when *know-why* or *know-how* knowledge can be applied and allows managers to make conjectures about what new kinds of products a firm might develop.

The danger in all this of course is that organizations learn from an overly narrow small product sample, compounded by wider uncertainty. The attraction of 'sticking to the knitting' is understandable in firms where resources are limited. However this 'core rigidity' or 'competency-trap' has its dangers (Michael and Palandjian, 2004, p. 270).

The immediately preceding three paragraphs create the illusion that WYM (and similar firms) are focused on 'market pull' for innovation. It is important to stretch that this is not always the case in innovative companies, and particularly we found evidence of 'technology push' at WYM. However, as we indicated earlier the question is one of balance, which often produces conflict. 'Pushing technology' as is often the case at WYM can and does lead to successful new products. However, the 'push' must be guided by the 'pull' of market and customer needs. It seems the conflict results in the matching process between technological attributes and customer needs (Adams, Day, and Dougherty, 1998).

Moreover 'matching' is essentially a bargaining process in which conflict is resolved within WYM's management team and between WYM and its suppliers and customers (Cyert and March, 1963; Gavetti, Levinthal, and Ocasio, 2007, p. 227).

Our observations and findings also further reinforce the role that organizational contexts play in managerial decision-making, especially in terms of the amount of information that is available or attended to by managers (Gavetti et al., 2007, p. 532). WYM's situational context (Gore, Banks, Millward, and Kyriakidou, 2006; Gore, Flin, Stanton, and Wong, 2015) influences new product development and production and more specific WYMs real-time market research heavily influences the manner in which they adopt new technologies and adapt in response to its context (Gavetti et al., 2007, pp. 532–533).

At least in the broad context of organizational learning as the dominant decision-making process, what we found was, despite the best endeavours of the general manager, the development of routines in new product development incurred strong resistance from the director of R&D (and co-owner). Whilst we found evidence of standardized practice in company documentation, the performance of product development seemed very different from what has been previously adopted in the literature (Gavetti et al., 2007, pp. 526–527).

To this point the discussion has dealt largely with organizational learning in a very broad sense. However, in our analysis we derived more detailed empirical concepts. Most of these are intimately linked with the predominant theoretical concept of organizational learning. However, they also offer empirical evidence of links between other elements of our theoretical framework. This discussion now deals with each of these empirically derived concepts and their relationship to existing theory and empirical evidence. The research questions appearing in brackets are the ones that provide the most evidence for the specific concept.

Improving process (RQ1b, RQ1c, RQ2b, RQ2c)

Process improvement is a commonly occurring concept across the copious product and operation management literature. It essentially refers to managerial activities and routines focused upon increased production or service efficiency. In our findings, it is evidenced in WYM's ongoing efforts to improve their production processes in pursuit of optimal production. At WYM, process improvement focused upon product development and operation and production scheduling. Our analysis reveals process improvement to be a theme that is common in linking decision-making with speed to market, decision-making with strategic flexibility, speed to market with sustainable outcomes and strategic flexibility with sustainable outcomes.

Production optimization through process improvement sounds, at least superficially, simple. However, the fact that it is linking so many of the theoretical concepts in our revised framework, infers something that is complex. Indeed a common, critique of 'performance improvement' initiatives is that they often failed to improve processes, and there is empirical evidence in support of this (Zellner, 2011). In line with our findings, it has been suggested that improving processes requires contextualized, coordinated and intensive management of knowledge in situ (Seethamraju and Marjanovic, 2009). If rather self-evident, it seems that local knowledge is vital if processes are to be improved.

Local knowledge is not simply about skilled 'know-how' (e.g. WYM's production workers are highly skilled textile mill operators). It is also about the development of relevant performance metrics focused on both people and processes. The aim is to find a balanced set of measures that aligns production performance with strategic aims and objectives (Amaratunga, Baldry, and Sarshar, 2001). Of course the development of so-called 'balanced scorecards' (Kaplan and Norton, 2001) as suggested immediately prior relies to an extent on having a relatively settled product line, production process and staff. In small enterprises particularly, as WYM exemplifies, settled production is generally the exception rather than the norm. Hence whilst broad routines may exist, there is considerable pressure to minimize the speed to market of new products. Elements of the production of such products are often not fully understood, affecting yields and production rates, requiring rapid and accurate learning, based on pragmatic, and balanced measurement of the performance of physical and human assets (Terwiesch and Bohn, 2001).

Improving technology (RQ1b, RQ1c, RQ2b, RQ2c)

Where process improvement implicitly focuses upon routines and people, this empirically derived concept of technology improvement focuses on technology. In a sense the concept is another lens for organizational learning and process improvement. As such it is perhaps no surprise that we found evidence of this concept in links between the same four theoretical concepts as process improvement (decision-making with speed to market, decision-making with strategic flexibility, speed to market with sustainable outcomes and strategic flexibility with sustainable outcomes).

The empirical grounding for technology improvement is evidenced in the ongoing efforts of WYM to improve, upgrade or acquire new technology. To do that WYM commissioned an engineering firm to provide the skills and expertise to improve, upgrade or acquire new production machinery. Technology improvement impacted positively upon the speed in which products reached the customers.

The evidence from WYM further confirms a wider proposition, that 'innovation is grounded in basic learning' developed through experimenting with different product formulation or design (Li, Li, Wang, and Ma, 2017; Yi, Gu, and Wei, 2017). Experiments such as these often test market reactions as much as technology (Alegre and Chiva, 2008). The overriding intent of adopting new or improved technology is to improve demand or customer service or the generation of production efficiencies (Edmondson, Winslow, Bohmer, and Pisano, 2003) again demonstrating a strong tie to process improvement. However production problems or issues may also stimulate the search for new technology (Greve, 2003, p. 687).

WYM is not unique in using 'technology push' to bring new products to customers. However, this assertive approach is balanced out by frequent consultation with customers. This is in line with previous findings of Adams et al. (1998) and reaffirms the importance of learning through real-time market research.

Technology improvement also requires careful timing. At WYM the upgrading of the specialty yarn machinery was planned and prioritized long before its actual planned date. Hence, WYM in conjunction with the engineering firm that carried out the upgrade set a date on the production board of the firm, where product orders were placed relative to the impending upgrade. This lends support to a more widely held contention that 'timing is everything' when it comes to investing in technology. This has been found to be especially true in the information technology (IT) investments, (as is the case at WYM). Rushed or premature investments are risky and may prove to be costly. Conversely, prevarication or delay may lead to a loss of competitiveness. Careful and considerate production capacity and technology planning is therefore key to optimizing technological investment, leading to improved resource management and optimized costs (Mukherji, Rajagopalan, and Tanniru, 2006). This of course must be linked to the release of new products that rely on new or improved production technology (Dai, Goodale, Byun, and Ding, 2018).

The increasing difficulty faced by many manufacturers is the widespread and ever-deepening use of information and communications technology (ICT) in production technologies. This overwhelming occurrence, as much as it promotes improved production, also promotes technological uncertainty in new or improved product development or manufacturing (Bstieler, 2005).There is a very real threat across all industries that new or breakthrough technologies might render existing products obsolete. Worse still even new products are not safe and may be overtaken before or shortly after the reach market. Hence speed to market is vital, but this must be tempered by good technological awareness.

Dealing with customer behaviours (RQ1a, RQ1b, RQ2a)

Customer or consumer behaviour is a substantial field of research. In the present context, we do not access the vast literature focused around marketing and psychology. In this work, customer behaviour refers to issues relating to decision-making and real-time market research, decision-making and speed to market, and real-time market research and financial sustainability (as per our revised theoretical framework).

In WYM 'dealing with customer behaviour' means working with customers in product development. This is common occurrence in strategic product development and enables firms to assess consumer preferences and develop products or services accordingly (Sanchez, 1996). However, although understanding customers or wider market preferences are critical to the successful development and production of new products or services, there may be issues associated with customers that pose significant challenges to new product development (Brozovic, 2018; Dai et al., 2018; Gärtner and Schön, 2016). Until these issues are understood, these firms may be hampered in their ability to bring innovativeness to market.

Not least of these challenges are time and resource pressures common in all modern firms (such as WYM). Firms may also have an unsupportive culture or have had prior experiences of the failure of new product introduction. More specifically, it has been found that the successful development or introduction of new products may be affected by firms ignoring or avoiding ambiguous market information. Instead of further refining their search, some firms faced with such an issue rely instead on their conventional established understanding of markets. Relating strongly to the inability or unwillingness to deal with ambiguity is a common habit of using market information only where it conforms to prior expectations. Such behaviours amplify the bounded rationality of firms, and exacerbate compartmentalized thinking within firms (Adams et al., 1998, p. 404).

It has been found that overcoming compartmentalization in product development requires the achievement of good balance between leadership management and autonomous problem solving by product development teams. This balance further depends upon a well-articulated and overarching mission (Brown and Eisenhardt, 1995, p. 359).

Further supporting our finding around the role of real-time market research, there is other evidence of the importance of strong ties between firms and their suppliers and wider research and development networks (Brown and Eisenhardt, 1995). WYM exemplify the value of feedback and collaborative links in their ability to work alongside their customers. Their intention is not just to exchange knowledge, but to earn trust and extend their product development team.

Referring back to the earlier theme of ignoring ambiguity in the market data and of compartmentalized thinking, there is evidence elsewhere to indicate that this is a means through which firms overcome misinterpretation of information (Adams et al., 1998). A common cliché in management texts is the importance of being 'comfortable with uncertainty'. In practice this is difficult and may be managed through a formal risk management system or informally through frequent discussion of challenges faced and possible solutions, accessing sources of information or accessing other forms of expertise. Predictive forecasting is also important (Cyert and March, 1992) but communication is key (Brozovic, 2018; Dai et al., 2018; Li et al., 2017; Luoma, 2016; Yang, Zhang, and Xie, 2017).

Harness market opportunities (RQ1a, RQ1b, RQ2a)

Focusing in further on the construct of real-time market research and its relationship with decision-making and financial sustainability, the empirical concept of harnessing market opportunities, also ties with decision-making and rapid performance upgrades (Brozovic, 2018; Dai et al., 2018; Gärtner and Schön, 2016; Li et al., 2017; Luoma, 2016; Yang et al., 2017; Yi et al., 2017).

Whilst market data can be problematic, as discussed in the previous section, it has been found that managers may benefit from paying careful attention to market trends (Sanchez, 1996). We found evidence that WYM follows this finding, and as for other firms, this enables them to organize and coordinate different or new kinds of product creation processes which significantly increases the scope for end rate of new product creation. This has its foundation in gathering and interpreting real-time market data.

Grounding new product creation ('technology push') in market and customer needs is more likely to lead to successful products because development activities are continuously guided by market information. Iterating between incremental improvement (push) and customer feedback (pull) enables matching of customer needs to technology design attributes (Adams et al., 1998). Developing incremental improvements relies on product experimentation as a basic means of learning, enabling innovation. Experimentation allows firms to test market and technology related issues (Alegre and Chiva, 2008). Findings from WYM support this. Exemplified by WYM, a robust product strategy involves decisions about the firm's target market and which product opportunities can be explored further. Also, it involves decisions around which technologies will be employed in the planned products. The strategic manager will then have to coordinate these decisions with the firm's corporate, marketing and operations strategies, approve the product plan (depending on how well it meets strategic goals), justify the product opportunity, and assess how well the target market fits the company's image and vision (Krishnan and Ulrich, 2001, p. 10).

Finally, as WYM's case shows, it is common for firms to enter multiple short- or long-term collaborations with other firms. This, rather like work intensification, could place the firms as network actuator under great pressure. However as is the case at WYM, this potential for intensity may be mitigated through identifying partners with complimentary capabilities and expertise in product development, manufacturing, distribution or marketing (Sanchez, 1996, p. 124).

Maintain a competitive advantage (RQ1c, RQ2c)

Picking up on the previous discussion, within a network of relationships, how may a firm maintain its distinctive 'edge'?

Our findings show that WYM aimed at maintaining a competitive advantage approach to some degree. For example, that happened when WYM involved themselves in discussions with a sheep breeders group to secure a sustainable supply chain of locally sourced raw wool. Their innovative technology to design and transform raw wool into specialty yarn is another example of WYM aiming to remain frontrunners and ahead of their competitors in this highly competitive market.

WYM's edge involves around it foundational wool treatment technology and incremental innovation in yarn production. The aim at WYM is to develop products that are not easily imitated and technology that is difficult to substitute. They also rely on highly skilled workers who often come from generations of skilled textile workers. Hence, in supporting theory relating to the resource-based view of the firm, WYM's resources are exploited and drive value creations in pursuit of competitive advantage (Sirmon, Hitt, and Ireland, 2007, p. 273). Strongly related to this is WYM's exemplification of the dynamic capabilities paradigm, whereby the management team carefully but dynamically manages the competencies embedded in its resources, rendering them distinctive, and enabling the company to survive, succeed and stand out from its competitors (Wang and Ahmed, 2007, p. 41). There is evidence that WYM in a limited manner is seeking to build values associated with environmental stewardship into the firm (Haropoulou, Smallman, and Radford, 2013; Hart, 1995; Marcus, 2009).

This is in line with the contention that one of the most important drivers of new resource and capability development for firms will be the constraints and challenges posed by the natural (biophysical) environment (Hart, 1995, p. 989; Perez-Valls, Cespedes-Lorente, and Moreno-Garcia, 2015). This in turn is arguably in line with the proposition that competitive advantage depends upon the match between distinctive internal (organizational) capabilities and changing external (environmental) circumstances (Fowler and Hope, 2007; Hart, 1995, p. 987). Taking this a little further given the origins of the present study, the natural environment has been identified as an important area for economic competition (Shrivastava, 1995). Ecological issues regarding energy, natural resources, pollution and waste offer both competitive opportunities as well as constraints, and are continuously changing the competitive landscape in many industries. Hence corporations can gain competitive advantage by managing ecological variables. This is in line with current thinking around the role of supply chains in ecological, economic production systems (Haropoulou et al., 2013) and extends to the use of 'environmental technologies' as a set of management techniques (technologies, equipment, operating procedures) that can be used to gain competitive advantage.

We also found in WYM further evidence to support validity of the concept of strategic flexibility (Brozovic, 2018; Dai et al., 2018; Gärtner and Schön, 2016; Li et al., 2017; Perez-Valls et al., 2015; Yi et al., 2017). This is founded on the flexibility of a firm's resources (resource flexibility) and the flexibility of the firm to use its available resources in product markets (coordination flexibility) (Sanchez, 1995, p. 135). We further argue that these two aspects of flexibility demonstrate the ability of a firm to sustain its competitive advantage. This is supported by earlier research that highlights the need for managers to employ strategic flexibility to respond to problems speedily. It is suggested that this is doubly important where there is a highly dynamic and changing environment. Furthermore it has been suggested that managers should be prepared to act to avoid rigidity and to adapt quickly to market dynamism (Shimizu and Hitt, 2004).

It has also been argued that the speed at which firms bring new products to market is considered a key component to achieving a competitive advantage (Sanchez, 2002, p. 11). Indeed new product development (NPD) speed has been seen as an increasingly important characteristic for managing innovation in fast changing business environments (Chen, Reilly, and Lynn, 2005, 2012). Moreover, it may be that speed becomes less important when uncertainty is low, but the opposite happens when there are conditions of extremely high uncertainty. However product quality also plays a role here as much as speed to market (Chen et al., 2005, pp. 12–13).

Our findings with respect to this concept evidence a link between both decision-making and strategic flexibility, and strategic flexibility and sustainable business outcomes.

Uncertainty in development (RQ1a)

Our findings suggest that there are uncertainties in product development, uncertainties surrounding the application of new or upgraded technologies and further risks associated with fluctuating market conditions. Moreover, risk increases when customers alter their product preferences without enough warning or when they exhibit challenging behaviours. To mitigate uncertainty, WYM actively engages in discussions with their supply chain partners, listens to their feedback and acts accordingly. In addition to that approach, WYM seeks and utilizes capabilities, strengths and expertise of other firms. This approach reaps great results when new product developments (NPD) are involved or other firms' capabilities are exploited.

The empirical concept of uncertainty in development offers a link between the following theoretical concepts: uncertainty avoidance and real-time market research, resolution of conflict and real-time market research, problemistic search and real-time market research and problemistic search and multiple firm collaborations.

This supports the empirical derived notion that while new product development is an important part of many firms operations, it can be a risky and uncertain process (Ozer, 2005). However, uncertainty is a common feature of organizational decision-making and organizations must learn to live with it and adapt.

Much of modern decision theory addresses the problem of decision-making under risk and uncertainty (Cyert and March, 1992, pp. 166–169) and the concept of strategic flexibility is directly related to a firm's response to managing uncertainty in the current product markets (Sanchez, 1995, pp. 137–140). It has also been argued that firms achieve a manageable decision situation through (a) feedback-react decision procedures where they avoid planning that depends on predicting an uncertain future and rather emphasizing on short-run reaction based on feedback from short-run problems and (b) negotiated environment where firms also make some predictions about the behaviour of their environment, especially the environment that is represented by competitors, suppliers, customers, and other parts of the organization (Cyert and March, 1992).

Such manageable decisions take a more realistic view in which individuals make decisions that are 'good enough', based on limited information and the knowledge they have (Luoma, 2016; March and Simon, 1958). This is now commonly known as cue-based or naturalistic decision-making (Gore, Banks, et al., 2006; Gore, Flin, et al., 2015; Shattuck and Miller, 2006).

A recurring theme in the theory around new product development and uncertainty is the identified need for careful evaluation of new product ideas, common as 'screening' (Hammedi, van Riel, and Sasovova, 2011; Ozer, 2005). In summary, the literature identifies a mix of managerial and technical decisions guided by decision tools and data (Hammedi et al., 2011; Ozer, 2005; Yahaya and Abu-Bakar, 2007). Decision-making tools based on data are focused upon handling issues associated with strategic management, project management, process and structure and people (Yahaya and Abu-Bakar, 2007) by helping managers to avoid the errors that go with assumption-laden decision-making. Balancing good leadership with skilled team work is a recurrent theme (Hammedi et al., 2011) and this is borne out in my findings. A further means of offsetting uncertainty is frequent interactions with customers through real-time market research (Sanchez and Sudharshan, 1993). Again, we found evidence to support this at WYM. At the other 'end' of the value chain, as we found at WYM, close involvement with suppliers is a further means of reducing uncertainty in NPD, especially with rapidly evolving technology (Ragatz, Handfield, and Petersen, 2002). As practiced by WYM, holding close relationships with suppliers both moderates risk and reduce the chances of NPD failing (Ragatz et al., 2002, p. 393). By including suppliers with the development team WYM reduces lead times and development costs, and to improve quality. This is in line with other findings (Ragatz et al., 2002, p. 398).

Problem solving and learning through collaborations (RQ1a)

Our findings support the notion that seeking other firms' capabilities is a key driver contributing to organizational learning. WYM uses firm collaborations to acquire additional development capabilities or perform various tests on product characteristics and production outcomes thereby increasing their product knowledge. Particularly when purchasing decisions (i.e. technology improvements, or new machinery acquisition), or product testing against various quality standards is involved, firm collaborations allow the use of complimentary capabilities in product development, manufacturing, distribution and marketing hence incrementing the company's knowledge in these areas.

Our findings are in line with a wide range of existing empirical findings and theory (Li et al., 2017). Part of this argument is that to obtain new or complement existing capabilities in product creation and acquire new market knowledge, a firm may enter *multiple* long-term or short-term *collaborations* with other firms. This way the pressure put upon the firm for faster product development can be alleviated through the use of complimentary capabilities and expertise in product development, manufacturing distribution or marketing (Sanchez, 1996, p. 124). This implicitly builds on the notion of problemistic search as a "search that is stimulated by a problem . . . and is directed toward finding a solution to that problem". As such problemistic search implies that organizational aspiration levels adapt to the past experience of the focal organization and those of comparable organizations (Argote and Greve, 2007, p. 343).

It has been suggested that organizations benefit more from the experience of other firms in the industry and less from their own experience as performance deviates from aspiration levels. This indicates that local search is stimulated by performance near aspiration levels, whereas non-local search follows as performance moves away from aspirations. Furthermore it seems that the absorptive capacity of a firm increases when its capabilities are combined more readily with those of an extensive network of developers (Sanchez and Mahoney, 2003, p. 372). Hence inter-firm relationships and supply chain collaboration activities become vehicles to improve new venture success and to leverage of resources and knowledge between suppliers and customers (Cao and Zhang, 2011; Lee, 2007; Wu and Cavusgil, 2006).

In WYM's chosen industry sector, companies must be experts not only in their in-house research, but also seek to undertake cooperative research with other external partners, such as universities, research organizations and, sometimes, competitors (Powell, Koput, and Smith-Doerr, 1996, p. 119). In many instances WYM sends samples of incoming raw sliver to a local research institute to test the length of the raw wool sliver. WYM and customers demand better product and nowadays in business markets, "customers are fundamentally changing the dynamics of the market place. The market has become a forum in which customers play an active role . . . in new product development" (Prahalad and Ramaswamy, 2000, p. 80).

Mitigating supply chain uncertainties (RQ1a)

Our findings indicate that uncertainty surrounding market instabilities (i.e. price fluctuation of raw materials, high New Zealand currency) is partly resolved through partnerships with other firms that can provide complimentary capabilities or raw materials.

Established theory explains how some firms react to uncertain market conditions (Brozovic, 2018; Dai et al., 2018; Gärtner and Schön, 2016; Li et al., 2017; Luoma, 2016; Sanchez, 1996; Yang et al., 2017). Because of the uncertainty about where technologies or market preferences are headed in the long term, firms choose to adopt a regime of 'fixed-asset parsimony'. Instead of acquiring specific-use assets which can be rigid and inflexible, investments are channelled into building intellectual assets like human knowledge and capabilities that is more flexible and can be leveraged in a variety of ways as market conditions change. Networking and other connections with other firms present another way of mitigating uncertainties. The notion of flexibility is important in mitigating supply chain uncertainty (Sanchez, 1996; Seethamraju and Marjanovic, 2009).

In their efforts to mitigate supply chain risks, many companies change their business models by adopting lean practices or by outsourcing part of their business or by reducing the supplier base. Hence as Christopher and Lee (2004) note, a key element in any strategy designed to mitigate supply chain risk is improved "end-to-end" visibility.

Chapter summary

The aim of this chapter was to form a discussion around our findings and how they link to existing body of literature. The discussion emerged from the revised theoretical framework presented in section 5.2. Based on this framework empirically derived concepts were outlined and for each one we cross referenced the relevant literature to provide theoretical support for our findings. Hence, we presented a range of concepts starting with the most highly referenced concept of organizational learning, and continuing with process and technology improvement, dealing with customer behaviours and harnessing market opportunities, maintaining a competitive advantage and highlighting the uncertainty in product development and finally the concepts of problem solving though collaborations and mitigating supply chain uncertainties. Some of these concepts appeared to have strong evidence in the findings while others less so.

In the next chapter, we undertake the task of providing some useful concluding comments for this research.

References

Adams, M. E., Day, G. S., and Dougherty, D. (1998). Enhancing new product development performance: An organizational learning perspective. *Journal of Product Innovation Management, 15*(5), 403–422.

Alegre, J., and Chiva, R. (2008). Assessing the impact of organizational learning capability on product innovation performance: An empirical test. *Technovation, 28*(6), 315–326.

Amaratunga, D., Baldry, D., and Sarshar, M. (2001). Process improvement through performance measurement: The balanced scorecard methodology. *International Journal of Productivity and Performance Management, 50*(5), 179–189. doi: 10.1108/EUM0000000005677.

Argote, L., and Greve, H. R. (2007). A behavioral theory of the firm – 40 years and counting: Introduction and impact. *Organization Science, 18*(3), 337–349. doi: 10.1287/orsc.1070.0280.

Brown, S. L., and Eisenhardt, K. M. (1995). Product development: Past research, present findings, and future directions. *Academy of Management, 20*(2), 343–378.

Brozovic, D. (2018). Strategic flexibility: A review of the literature. *International Journal of Management Reviews, 20*(1), 3–31.

Bstieler, L. (2005). The moderating effect of environmental uncertainty on new product development and time efficiency. *Journal of Product Innovation Management, 22*(3), 267–284. doi: 10.1111/j.0737–6782.2005.00122.x.

Caemmerer, B., and Wilson, A. (2010). Customer feedback mechanisms and organisational learning in service operations. *International Journal of Operations & Production Management, 30*(3), 288–311. doi: 10.1108/01443571011024638.

Cao, M., and Zhang, Q. (2011). Supply chain collaboration: Impact on collaborative advantage and firm performance. *Journal of Operations Management, 29*(3), 163–180.

Chen, J., Reilly, R. R., and Lynn, G. S. (2005). *Uncertainty: Is it a threat or opportunity for new product development teams?* Retrieved from http://isbm.smeal.psu.edu/library/working-paper-articles/2005-working-papers/18-2005 Uncertainty Is it a Threat or Opportunity for New Product Development Teams.pdf

Chen, J., Reilly, R. R., and Lynn, G. S. (2012). New product development speed: Too much of a good thing? *Journal of Product Innovation Management, 29*(2), 288–303.

Christopher, M., and Lee, H. (2004). Mitigating supply chain risk through improved confidence. *International Journal of Physical Distribution & Logistics Management, 34*(5), 388–396.

Cyert, R. M., and March, J. G. (1963). *A behavioral theory of the firm*. New Jersey: Prentice-Hall Inc.

Cyert, R. M., and March, J. G. (1992). *A behavioral theory of the firm*. New Jersey: Prentice-Hall Inc.

Dai, Y., Goodale, J. C., Byun, G., and Ding, F. (2018). Strategic flexibility in new high-technology ventures. *Journal of Management Studies, 55*(2), 265–294.

Edmondson, A. C., Winslow, A. B., Bohmer, R. M. J., and Pisano, G. P. (2003). Learning how and learning what: Effects of tacit and codified knowledge on performance improvement following technology adoption. *Decision Sciences, 34*(2), 197–223.

Fowler, S. J., and Hope, C. (2007). Incorporating sustainable business practices into company strategy. *Business Strategy and the Environment, 16*(1), 26–38. doi: 10.1002/bse.462.

Gärtner, C., and Schön, O. (2016). Modularizing business models: Between strategic flexibility and path dependence. *Journal of Strategy and Management, 9*(1), 39–57.

Gavetti, G., Levinthal, D., and Ocasio, W. (2007). Neo-Carnegie: The Carnegie school's past, present, and reconstructing for the future. *Organization Science, 18*(3), 523–536.

Golden-Biddle, K., and Locke, K. (2007). *Composing qualitative research.* Thousand Oaks, CA: Sage.

Gore, J., Banks, A., Millward, L., and Kyriakidou, O. (2006). Naturalistic decision-making and organisations: Reviewing pragmatic science. *Organization Studies, 27*(7), 925–942.

Gore, J., Flin, R., Stanton, N., and Wong, B. L. W. (2015). Editorial: Applications for naturalistic decision-making. *Journal of Occupational and Organizational Psychology, 88*, 223–230.

Greve, H. R. (2003). A behavioral theory of R&D expenditures and innovations: Evidence from shipbuilding. *The Academy of Management Journal, 46*(6), 685–702.

Hammedi, W., van Riel, A. C. R., and Sasovova, Z. (2011). Antecedents and consequences of reflexivity in new product idea screening. *Journal of Product Innovation Management, 28*(5), 662–679. doi: 10.1111/j.1540–5885.2011.00831.x.

Haropoulou, M., Smallman, C., and Radford, J. (2013). Supply chain management and the delivery of ecosystems services in manufacturing. In S. Wratten, H. Sandu, R. Cullen, and R. Costanza (Eds.), *Ecosystems services in agricultural and urban landscapes* (pp. 157–177). John Wiley & Sons.

Hart, S. L. (1995). A natural resource based view of the firm. *Academy of Management Review, 20*(4), 986–1014.

Kaplan, R. S., and Norton, D. P. (2001). Transforming the balanced scorecard from performance measurement to strategic management: Part I. *Accounting Horizons, 15*(1), 87–104. doi: 10.2308/acch.2001.15.1.87.

Krishnan, V., and Ulrich, K. T. (2001). Product development decisions: A review of the literature. *Management Science, 47*(1), 1–21.

Lee, C.-W. (2007). Strategic alliances influence on small and medium firm performance. *Journal of Business Research, 60*(7), 731–741.

Levitt, B., and March, J. G. (1988). Organizational learning. *Annual Review of Sociology, 14*, 319–340.

Li, Y., Li, P. P., Wang, H., and Ma, Y. (2017). How do resource structuring and strategic flexibility interact to shape radical innovation? *Journal of Product Innovation Management, 34*(4), 471–491.

Luoma, J. (2016). Model-based organizational decision making: A behavioral lens. *European Journal of Operational Research, 249*(3), 816–826.

March, J. G., and Simon, H. A. (1958). *Organisations.* New York: Wiley.

Marcus, A. A. (2009). Strategic direction and management. In R. Staib (Ed.), *Business management and environmental stewardship* (pp. 38–55). Basingstoke, UK: Palgrave MacMillan.

Michael, S. C., and Palandjian, T. P. (2004). Organizational learning and new product introductions. *Journal of Product Innovation Management, 21*(4), 268–276. doi: 10.1111/j.0737–6782.2004.00078.x.

Mukherji, N., Rajagopalan, B., and Tanniru, M. (2006). A decision support model for optimal timing of investments in information technology upgrades. *Decision Support Systems, 42*(3), 1684–1696.

Ozer, M. (2005). Factors which influence decision making in new product evaluation. *European Journal of Operational Research, 163*(3), 784–801.

Perez-Valls, M., Cespedes-Lorente, J., and Moreno-Garcia, J. (2015). Green practices and organizational design as sources of strategic flexibility and performance. *Business Strategy and the Environment, 25*(8).

Powell, W. W., Koput, K. W., and Smith-Doerr, L. (1996). Interorganizational collaboration and the locus of innovation: Networks of learning in biotechnology. *Administrative Science Quarterly, 41*(1), 116–145.

Prahalad, C. K., and Ramaswamy, V. (2000). Co-opting customer competence (Brief Article). *Harvard Business Review, 78*(1), 78–87.

Ragatz, G. L., Handfield, R. B., and Petersen, K. J. (2002). Benefits associated with supplier integration into new product development under conditions of technology uncertainty. *Journal of Business Research, 55*(5), 389–400.

Sanchez, R. (1995). Strategic flexibility in product competition. *Strategic Management Journal, 16*, 135–159.

Sanchez, R. (1996). Strategic product creation: Managing new interactions of technology, markets, and organizations. *European Management Journal, 14*(2), 121–138. doi: 10.1016/0263-2373(95)00056-9.

Sanchez, R. (2002). Using modularity to manage the interactions of technical and industrial design. *Design Management Journal, 2*(1), 8–19.

Sanchez, R., and Mahoney, J. T. (2003). Modularity, flexibility, and knowledge management in product and organization design. In *Managing in modular age: Architectures, networks, and organizations* (pp. 362–389). Blackwell Publishers.

Sanchez, R., and Sudharshan, D. (1993). Real-time market research. *Marketing Intelligence & Planning, 11*(7), 29–38.

Seethamraju, R., and Marjanovic, O. (2009). Role of process knowledge in business process improvement methodology: A case study. *Business Process Management Journal, 15*(6), 920–936.

Shattuck, L. G., and Miller, N. L. (2006). Extending naturalistic decision making to complex organisations: A dynamic model situated cognition. *Organization Studies, 27*(7), 989–1010.

Shimizu, K., and Hitt, M. A. (2004). Strategic flexibility: Organizational preparedness to reverse ineffective strategic decisions. *The Academy of Management Executive (1993–2005), 18*(4), 44–59.

Shrivastava, P. (1995). Environmental technologies and competitive advantage. *Strategic Management Journal, 16*(S1), 183–200. doi: 10.1002/smj.4250160923.

Sirmon, D. G., Hitt, M. A., and Ireland, D. R. (2007). Managing firm resources in dynamic environments to create value: Looking inside the black box. *Academy of Management Review, 32*(1), 273–292. doi: 10.5465/amr.2007.23466005.

Slater, S. F., and Narver, J. C. (1995). Market orientation and the learning organization. *Journal of Marketing, 59*(3), 63–63.

Terwiesch, C., and Bohn, R. E. (2001). Learning and process improvement during production ramp-up. *International Journal of Production Economics, 70*(1), 1–19.

Wang, C. L., and Ahmed, P. K. (2007). Dynamic capabilities: A review and research agenda. *International Journal of Management Reviews, 9*(1), 31–51. doi: 10.1111/j.1468-2370.2007.00201.x.

Wu, F., and Cavusgil, S. T. (2006). Organizational learning, commitment, and joint value creation in interfirm relationships. *Journal of Business Research, 59*(1), 81–89.

Yahaya, S.-Y., and Abu-Bakar, N. (2007). New product development management issues and decision-making approaches. *Management Decision, 45*(7), 1123–1123. doi: 10.1108/00251740710773943.

Yang, Z., Zhang, H., and Xie, E. (2017). Performance feedback and supplier selection: A perspective from the behavioral theory of the firm. *Industrial Marketing Management, 63*, 105–115.

Yi, Y., Gu, M., and Wei, Z. (2017). Bottom-up learning, strategic flexibility and strategic change. *Journal of Organizational Change Management, 30*(2), 161–183.

Zellner, G. (2011). A structured evaluation of business process improvement approaches. *Business Process Management Journal, 17*(2), 203–237. doi: 10.1108/14637151111122329.

6 Conclusions

This book links together three bodies of literature: the behavioural theory of the firm (Cyert and March, 1992; March and Simon, 1993; Simon, 1997), strategic product creation (Sanchez, 1995, 1996, 2002; Sanchez and Mahoney, 1996) and sustainable business outcomes (Dunphy, Griffiths, and Benn, 2007).

The journey for this study started soon after we completed a life cycle assessment (LCA) report for a New Zealand wool yarn manufacturer (WYM) who wanted to assess their environmental footprint. The company's owner John, with his inherent ambition to improve processes and products and in a more sustainable fashion, was curious to find out whether the LCA report could be used as a starting point for shaping organizational decisions around their product development processes in a way that incorporates sound sustainable practices. That is aiming to reduce further the firm's environmental impact without minimizing their financial benefits or adversely impacting upon the company's staff or stakeholders. Coupled with our interests in the area of sustainable business practices, the following research question was formulated:

> "How do organizational decisions around new product development affect sustainable business outcomes?"

And hence the journey of this study began. We started by reviewing the behavioural theory of decision-making processes, followed by the strategic product creation and the business sustainability theories. Hence, this book links together three bodies of literature: the behavioural theory of the firm (Cyert and March, 1992; March and Simon, 1993; Simon, 1997), strategic product creation (Sanchez, 1995, 1996, 2002; Sanchez and Mahoney, 1996) and sustainable business outcomes (Dunphy et al., 2007). We concluded our review with a theoretical synthesis and the development of a conceptual framework combining the three theories together. Based on the synthesized theoretical model we were able to further develop six research questions.

We adopted a single-case study research strategy and one of us entered the firm (WYM) as an observer gathering 'rich' information and people perceptions through inductive, qualitative analysis based on discussions, participant observations, unstructured interviews, and document analysis. We followed the company for seven months by which time we had a rich data set comprised of data transcribed from meetings, interviews, observations and documents analysis. We then used computer software for the qualitative analysis.

Our initial approach to data analysis proved to be rather challenging. More specifically, some issues surfaced around the well-known argument of 'intercoder reliability' (Miles and Huberman, 1994), a measure of agreement among multiple coders on how they apply codes to text data. When an attempt was made to codify samples of our data from two independent researchers the results produced were ambiguous.

These challenges led us to explore a different approach and to perform further analysis, which ensured rigour in our research. Following the recommendations of Rynes and Gephart (2004) the second qualitative analysis software tool we used was a computer-aided textual analysis tool (Leximancer), which allowed a systematic, comprehensive and unbiased re-analysis of the data. As mentioned previously, the aim of this study was to establish links among three theories and to do so we articulated six research questions which linked decision-making to strategic product creation practices and then linked strategic product creation practices to sustainable business outcomes theories. We disaggregated each research question to its basic theoretical concepts and was able to identify co-existence of concepts from different theories in the same piece of analyzed text hence links among the three theories.

Through a systematic analysis of the data collected at the case study organization we derived a range of empirical concepts:

1   Learning from feedback
2   Improving process
3   Improving technology
4   Dealing with customer behaviours
5   Harness market opportunities
6   Maintain a competitive advantage
7   Uncertainty in development
8   Problem solving and learning through collaborations
9   Mitigating supply chain uncertainties

We also found some strong, moderate and weak links among all theoretical concepts.

By far the strongest relationship was found to be between the decision-making theoretical concept of organizational learning and the product creation concept of real-time market research. This strong link indicates that across all product creation processes WYM mostly applied feedback mechanisms incorporated in the theoretical concept of real-time research to enhance or generate new knowledge.

Another reasonably strong link was found between organizational learning and the product strategy theoretical concept of speed to market which is key business performance indicator monitoring production efficiencies and identifying how fast manufactured products can be delivered to the customer.

Across all central strategy processes some links existed between organizational learning and fixed asset parsimony and between organizational learning and strategic flexibility. These links indicate the desire of WYM to learn, improve their product development practices and be flexible enough and adapt to changing market conditions.

When we linked the product creation, product strategy and central strategy constructs to the business sustainability outcomes there was some evidence that real-time market research impacts mostly upon the financial element of sustainability. There was limited evidence that speed to market improved the financial performance of the company. At the end of the spectrum the central strategy concepts showed little or no impact upon the business sustainability outcomes.

RQ1a. How do decision-making processes affect product creation processes? Organizational learning contributes to product creation processes in enabling learning from feedback, countering uncertainty, dealing with customer behaviours and harnessing market opportunities. These concepts are all elements of real-time market research.

RQ1b. How do decision-making processes affect product strategy processes? Organizational learning contributes to product strategy in the form of dealing with customer behaviours or when improving production processes and technology. What these concepts enable is improved speed to market.

RQ1c: How do decision-making processes affect central strategy processes? Organizational learning contributes to central (firm) strategy in the form of process improvement, technology enhancement and in maintaining competitive advantage. This enables WYM to affect parsimony in investment in fixed assets whilst leveraging their considerable intellectual assets.

RQ2a: How do product creation processes affect business sustainability outcomes? In contrast to previous research questions, there is far less evidence that links product creation processes to the business sustainability outcomes. The real-time market research concept only partly affects the environmental and financial elements of sustainability when dealing with customers' behaviours or when investigating market opportunities further. We found no evidence of a connection between the multiple collaborations concept and the business sustainability outcomes.

RQ2b: How do product strategy processes affect business sustainability outcomes? The product strategy concepts have limited impact on the sustainability outcomes. More specifically speed to market and financial sustainability is mostly evidenced when technology or production process improvements take place. There is no evidence that the two remaining concepts of rapid performance upgrade and proliferation of product variety impact upon business sustainability outcomes.

RQ2c: How do central strategy processes affect business sustainability outcomes? There is very little evidence that links central strategy processes to the business sustainability outcomes. A limited number of references link the strategic flexibility theoretical concept to the environmental and financial elements of sustainability. There is no evidence linking fixed asset parsimony or modular product architecture theoretical concepts to business sustainability.

Contributions

Contribution to theory

Our findings reinforce again the importance and role of organizational learning in organizational decision-making. This goes against recent critique of the Carnegie organizational research tradition, which argues that the focus of much of the research that follows the tradition is too narrowly focused on organizational learning. However, our findings were generated from data rather than through hypothesis testing. Hence our focus was not on organizational learning as such, but rather emerged from a novel approach to data analysis.

As such one of our contributions is to challenge the view that decision-making research has given way to organizational learning research. Rather, in our approach, organizational learning emerged as a dominant theme. We argue that our findings further contribute to the argument that organizations are "shaped by, but not reducible to, human behaviours social relations or market and . . . environments" (Gavetti, Levinthal, and Ocasio, 2007, p. 523).

We believe that we have further confirmed the long held view that decision-making is almost the singularly important activity that takes place in organization (Cyert and March, 1992; March and Simon, 1993; Simon, 1997).

We have also further contributed to the Carnegie's conventional wisdom that behavioural realism is vital in theory building. Our observations at WYM certainly involved watching people's behaviours in the real world, and my findings are firmly grounded in those observations as much if not more so, as in the theoretical framework we developed and revised.

What our findings further suggest is the importance of developing a more comprehensive understanding of situational context on decision-making. No better example of this exists in our findings around the links between organizational learning and real-time market research. The impact of organizational environment is crucial in a business such as WYM is (Gavetti et al., 2007, p. 528).

To a limited extent, based on our observations of decision-handling in various meetings, we also support and contribute to the call for "renewal attention to the consequences of structure on organizational actions and outcomes" (Gavetti et al., 2007, p. 532).

In terms of theory focused on strategic product creation (Sanchez, 1996), we were initially frustrated by lack of precision in the manner in which at least some of the theory was conceptualized. In synthesizing our theoretical framework, we believe we have contributed to this lack of theory by 'tightening' the definition and merging several concepts. Our findings suggest that further narrowing of the scope of this theory may be possible.

We also believe that we have contributed to further understanding the link between decision-making and new product development. We have found evidence that WYM is a proactive learning organization that operates under conditions of uncertainty with bounded rationality and imperfect knowledge (Pitelis, 2007, p. 483). We have further found that intra-firm decision-making and resources are very important (witnessed WYM's relationship with its customers and suppliers). Moreover our findings enhance the theoretical position that firms change dynamically in response to their environment (product innovation), and that such change drives, at least in part, the growth and performance of the firms (Pitelis, 2007, p. 483).

Certainly we have made a contribution to further confirming the resource-based view (RVB) paradigm's position that the possession of rare, valuable or imitable resources form the basis for competitive advantage (Sirmon, Hitt, and Ireland, 2007, p. 273). We have also documented how at least one firm 'transform[s] resources to create value', so further, if not implicitly elaborating the RBV (Sirmon et al., 2007, p. 273).

We have further developed the understanding of how 'highly effective coordinating processes facilitate the development of more creative and flexible capability configurations' ((Sirmon et al., 2007, p. 285) citing Sanchez (1995)).

Of the entire literature we used in this study, where we have made the least contribution is paradoxically where we were expecting to make the most: sustainability. However, whilst we may have done little to advance theoretical perspectives on social and ecological sustainability, we argue that the identified links to financial sustainability are important. More often than not, the importance of financial sustainability in business is lost in a well-meant rhetoric around 'greening' and stakeholders. Our modest contribution here, we argue is to reaffirm the point that 'doing good' starts from staying in business and making a profit, provided of course that in turning a profit the overriding principle should be *primum non nocere* ('first do no harm').

Looking across disciplinary boundaries, we made a contribution to theory that stresses the importance of strategic flexibility in decision-making for new product development (Kandemir and Acur, 2012). We add further evidence to support the position of how crucial flexibility is in decision-making. The importance of 'champions' and 'gatekeepers' is further supported (Kandemir and Acur, 2012).

Overall our contribution to theory rests on further establishing the links between three literatures which previously have enjoyed only a weak relationship. Hence based on the immediately preceding paragraphs, we believe that we have further developed the knowledge around the relationship between organizational decision-making, strategic product creation and business sustainability. Our exploratory approach has we believe yielded a number of contributions to the prior art.

Methodological contribution

The use of Leximancer in management research remains comparatively rare. By using this software, we have largely offset one of the conventional shortcomings of qualitative research: investigator bias.

The approach that we adopted took us "out of the equation" by basing lexicographic analysis of data based on words (and synonyms) held in theoretically defined concepts. Hence, we were able to allow ideas to 'grow' from data without overly influencing their derivation. This is we believe is a small but important contribution to analysis in this type of study.

Sustainability from the perspective of an innovative SME: observations of the practice of decision-making and new product development

The findings linking product creation practices to sustainable business outcomes were minimal. While the financial aspect of sustainability appeared to be mostly invoked around concepts of real-time market research and speed to market, the environmental impact of the product creation practices were minimal. Moreover, there was no indication that the social aspect of sustainability existed at WYM. All that said our observations and the picture we painted from one of us being an embedded researcher for seven months is worth mentioning here.

Although the findings around sustainable business practices were not encouraging, there were signs of minimizing the environmental footprint, saving energy and water usage and looking into the social aspect of sustainable practices that we noticed while we were collecting our data. For example, the installation of the pellet burner that was heating the water for the specialty treatment of the yarn was a major innovation project and WYM was the first company to undertake that sort of project on a commercial scale. Until then the application of wood pellet burners was mostly visible in the residential sector alone. Indeed, this innovative technology earned the company an award for using a renewable energy source.

The firm was keen to improve upon their existing practices, and this is where the business initiative of 'competitive manufacturing' played a substantial role. Not only it aimed to make processes run smoother, it was also designed to improve practices from an environmental and social aspect making the work place a desirable place to be.

We witnessed several discussions involving the WYM management and a sheep breeders group to innovate and produce a supply chain that would benefit both parties: WYM with a constant supply of wool and the supplier with a constant customer and both with a story of tracing where the wool fibre is coming from.

The firm was constantly on the lookout to improve, innovate and create a highly differentiated product that would be very attractive among their customers and difficult to copy among their competitors. The general manager often conveyed what was happening to the staff and was keen to maintain a two-way communication with an open-door policy to his office. Walkabouts in the factory were a common occurrence and the staff were made to feel valued by everyone. All-in-all WYM seemed to be a good place to work.

Future research

This research illustrates the richness of data that may be generated in a single-case study. Adding further value to this work would involve the development of further case studies in similar firms. However, this work took place over a limited time span. As past work on innovation demonstrates, there is much theoretical value to be gained in understanding lengthy studies of innovation processes such as we witnessed (Langley, Van de Ven, Smallman, and Tsoukas, 2013; Poole, Van de Ven, Dooley, and Holmes, 2000). It is a pity that governments worldwide invest heavily in innovation but not in developing an understanding of the process of innovation.

Whilst some authorities have rebelled against the need for further research in organizational learning (Gavetti et al., 2007), further research of the link between organizational learning and strategic flexibility is required. It has been previously suggested that there is a need to further develop the knowledge of the effects of situational context in decision-making, grounded in the naturalistic decision-making paradigm (Gore, Banks, Millward, and Kyriakidou, 2006).

Our limited findings suggest that further research in that area may be of value in furthering the development of a 'behaviourally plausible' theory of firm decision-making (Gavetti et al., 2007).

We also suggest that future researchers would benefit from further exploiting the analytical opportunities available in lexicographical analysis through Leximancer. More specifically using the 'discovery' mode of Leximancer may offer novel insights.

Closing observations

We started this book in recalling our first encounter with the issue of "environmental management for small and medium-sized enterprises (SMEs)" nearly thirty years ago in West Yorkshire in the north of England. Looking back to that time, whilst there has been progress, the central issue it seems to us remains largely unaltered and relates to John's question about connecting sustainability to SMEs: *anecdotally, many small businesses remain unable or unwilling to account for sustainability in their operations.* This is partly understandable in the global economic context of late 2018, but in the long-term this poses a substantial challenge for society, given the vast economic and social role that small businesses play across the developed and developing world.

References

Cyert, R. M., and March, J. G. (1992). *A behavioral theory of the firm.* New Jersey: Prentice-Hall Inc.

Dunphy, D., Griffiths, A., and Benn, S. (2007). *Organizational change for corporate sustainability: A guide for leaders and change agents of the future.* New York: Routledge.

Gavetti, G., Levinthal, D., and Ocasio, W. (2007). Neo-Carnegie: The Carnegie school's past, present, and reconstructing for the future. *Organization Science*, *18*(3), 523–536.

Gore, J., Banks, A., Millward, L., and Kyriakidou, O. (2006). Naturalistic decision-making and organisations: Reviewing pragmatic science. *Organization Studies*, *27*(7), 925–942.

Kandemir, D., and Acur, N. (2012). Examining proactive strategic decision-making flexibility in new product development. *Journal of Product Innovation Management*, n/a–n/a. doi: 10.1111/j.1540–5885.2012.00928.x.

Langley, A., Van de Ven, A. H., Smallman, C., and Tsoukas, H. (2013). Introduction to the special issue. *Academy of Management (in press)*.

March, J. G., and Simon, H. A. (1993). *Organisations* (2nd ed.). Cambridge, MA: Blackwell Publishers.

Miles, M. B., and Huberman, A. M. (1994). *Qualitative data analysis*. Sage.

Pitelis, C. N. (2007). A behavioral resource-based view of the firm: The synergy of cyert and march (1963) and penrose (1959). *Organization Science, 18*(3), 478–490.

Poole, M. S., Van de Ven, A. H., Dooley, K., and Holmes, M. E. (2000). *Organizational change and innovation processes*. New York: Oxford University Press.

Rynes, S., and Gephart, R. P. (2004). From the editors: Qualitative research and the "Academy of Management Journal". *The Academy of Management Journal, 47*(4), 454–462.

Sanchez, R. (1995). Strategic flexibility in product competition. *Strategic Management Journal, 16*, 135–159.

Sanchez, R. (1996). Strategic product creation: Managing new interactions of technology, markets, and organizations. *European Management Journal, 14*(2), 121–138.

Sanchez, R. (2002). Using modularity to manage the interactions of technical and industrial design. *Design Management Journal, 2*(1), 8–19.

Sanchez, R., and Mahoney, J. T. (1996). Modularity, flexibility, and knowledge management in product and organization design. *Strategic Management Journal, 17*(Winter Special Issue), 63.

Simon, H. A. (1997). *Administrative behaviour* (4th ed.). New York: The Free Press.

Sirmon, D. G., Hitt, M. A., and Ireland, D. R. (2007). Managing firm resources in dynamic environments to create value: Looking inside the black box. *Academy of Management Review, 32*(1), 273–292. doi: 10.5465/amr.2007.23466005.

Index

For Product Safety Concerns and Information please contact our EU
representative GPSR@taylorandfrancis.com
Taylor & Francis Verlag GmbH, Kaufingerstraße 24, 80331 München, Germany